The Nature of Marketing: A Comprehensive Marketing Guide for Natural Healthcare Providers

Bradley Jerome Johnson

Published by Bradley Jerome Johnson, 2023.

While every precaution has been taken in the preparation of this book, the publisher assumes no responsibility for errors or omissions, or for damages resulting from the use of the information contained herein.

THE NATURE OF MARKETING: A COMPREHENSIVE MARKETING GUIDE FOR NATURAL HEALTHCARE PROVIDERS

First edition. September 14, 2023.

ISBN: 979-8223779063

Written by Bradley Jerome Johnson.

Table of Contents

This book is dedicated to my brilliant wife, Dr. Jill Johnson, ND. Our journey together fills these pages with the stories I hope others can benefit from. You are my best friend, inspiration, and guide.

PREFACE

Is there anything more annoying than a self-proclaimed marketing expert? Marketers love to tell you they are marketers! Chances are you've been approached, cornered, or had a conversation hijacked by someone claiming to have the key to solving your business problems. With a fondness for using marketing jargon to confuse us, you'll be swept away by such fascinating terms as B2B, B2C, Lead Nurturing, KPIs, ROI, CRM, and A/B Split Testing - all taught in most undergraduate business programs and designed to build a shared vernacular among themselves and to confuse the rest of us into paying big dollars for their services.

My path to holistic marketing has been circuitous, and it has taken me a long time to accept my dirty little secret. I like marketing. I enjoy creating community, building relationships, and connecting people, which is at the heart of holistic marketing.

I believe conventional marketing over-relies upon data-driven analytics and metrics in decision-making. While having a solid understanding of your customers, prospective customers, their demographics, click-through rates, and analytics is an integral part of that understanding, it is also exceptionally limiting and lacks heart. As it looked to "science" for answers related to squishy human behavior, such as what motivates someone to buy Product A vs. Product B, the business world leaned into statistics and models of persuasion and created marketing systems based on the efforts of successful companies. It's hard to argue against the success of the large multinational corporations that bring in billions of dollars annually. But, like you, our businesses are not global nor have billion-dollar budgets, so what are we to do given the current state of marketing and reliance on a copy-paste type system?

What's lacking is a connection, a real connection with our customers, patients, or clients built over time with intention. Just because a marketing practice is common doesn't mean it is suitable for your business or is effective. It's essential to consider the kind of business you have or want to build. Your purpose and practice should be in alignment.

Unfortunately, we frequently see emulation through copy-paste; that is, we emulate the latest trends and essentially use a copy-and-paste approach. The copy-paste mentality is so typical these days that finding creative, innovative, and fresh ideas is challenging when visiting websites, viewing social media channels, and reading advertisement copy. New marketers and business owners often fall prey to just doing instead of "Doing with Intention." I often see this in social media posts when a popular meme emerges.

For example, everyone jumps on the bandwagon, replicating the original (and initially eye-catching) video post, replacing pop-up bubbles with fresh words, pointing at those word bubbles, and shrugging away with a smile at the end. These sorts of social media postings have a degree of cuteness, at least initially. Still, repeated attempts using the same practice yield little return and quickly become tired and dull. So doing is appealing because it *feels* like we are doing marketing and building our brand; instead, we are Doing Without Intention, and that's just busy work keeping us from other important tasks that can bring customers, clients, and patients into our business. I love this perspective from my wife, Dr. Jill Johnson, ND - the guiding principle behind her Blue Earth Medicine naturopathic medical practice is to "make more money to help more people." Unfortunately, many folks think the other way around, wanting to get more patients to make more money. That leads many to lose focus, question their abilities, and often shift their attention away from practice to start a program or begin another degree.

Setting up a business or medical practice or writing a book can lead to self-doubt, insecurity, and frustration. Of course, that's normal and to be expected, but it is not fun or fulfilling - quite the opposite. Each morning when I first wake, I wonder, "Will the words come today" and each day, I'm surprised to find the word-well is still flowing, some days better than others, of course. Some days I am nearly paralyzed with self-doubt, but I still get up, hit the computer, follow my outline and write. There are days when the words are bursting to get out of my head and other days when they trickle. During difficult times, instead of fretting about my word count for the day, I pivot and edit an earlier section. Each day it's essential to ask yourself, "Does this path still resonate with me?" or "Do I love what I'm doing?" - for me, the answer is yes. So I continue.

Life often takes us down paths we may not have expected or wanted. Still, these paths have opened up fascinating opportunities for personal and professional growth. My father passed away when I was just eight years old, which profoundly impacted my worldview and psychology. Growing up in a small Michigan factory town, I had limited options and barely graduated from high school. I struggled as a student, but I met a wonderful woman who inspired me to join the US Navy and prove my worth.

I trained as a cryptologist in the Navy and was stationed in Anchorage, Alaska. I chased Morse Code signals (we called them "dits and dahs") and decoded messages for four exciting years. However, I soon realized that higher education was essential for my career advancement and personal fulfillment. Therefore, I enrolled in a local community college and quickly became hooked on learning. This realization led me to leave the Navy and embark on a long, rewarding academic career.

Throughout my university years, I enjoyed learning about new subjects and dabbled in meteorology, aviation (earned my private pilot license), geography (earned my bachelor of science degree), parks and recreation administration (earned my master of art degree), and natural resource social science (spent four years in a Ph.D. program). During these years, I amassed a tremendous amount of scientific knowledge, social science acumen, and deep knowledge about research methods and statistics; later, I earned a certificate in enology and became a winemaker. Oddly enough, these disparate experiences coalesced and have enriched my professional development over the years.

My first experience with marketing occurred when I was in the US Navy as a writer and editor of the command newsletter. I loved writing creative and informative stories that were shared with other commands. However, during college, the business courses I took bored me to tears, so I shifted my attention to the field of parks and recreation, where I found my people. In this program, I learned everything from marketing, public relations, grant writing, communications, and program and event management, and it was a hoot! These skills have been transferable to every position I've held ever since.

I've enjoyed such diverse professional roles, such as executive director of nonprofit organizations and college instructor of psychology; in the wine industry, as external relations manager, digital marketing manager, marketing and communications manager, marketing and community relations manager; and also as a marketing consultant and now as a marketing coach. It's been a fun ride so far! So, Brad, what brought you to where you are at this point in your life?

Due to economic factors, I was unexpectedly released from my job in the wine industry in 2022. I'd never lost a job before, and the news hit me hard, leaving me questioning my self-worth. The good thing was that I was comfortable in dynamic situations. I took a few months to take stock and think about ways to reinvent myself, fortunately this wasn't my first time. We'd moved to Seattle in 2016 so my wife could make a mid-career change and begin training as a naturopathic doctor (ND) at one of the best naturopathic colleges in the nation, Bastyr University. I became acquainted with several NDs, professors, and students during this period. It was enjoyable learning, at least peripherally, about naturopathic medicine and seeing how natural medicine practices worked. However, I was most curious about how new naturopathic doctors found their way after graduation. Unlike conventional medical schools with specialties and residency programs and a well-established system, ND schools have fewer options. So many new ND graduates either seek out one of only a few residency opportunities, find a job with a clinic, or start a practice.

What initially caught my attention was the disappointingly poor quality of business training students received while in medical school; later on, I was shocked to hear about how some practices would hire new doctors at meager wages and hefty workloads. Other new doctors would fall prey to unscrupulous practice owners renting space for exorbitant rates, skimming revenue, and treating them like indentured servants. Likewise, I became increasingly irritated to hear stories from friends and colleagues about coaches and consulting businesses bilking thousands of dollars from them. So, after repeatedly hearing horror stories from practitioners about ineffective coaches and shady business owners, I became more interested in helping natural healthcare providers launch and market their businesses; thus, Brad Johnson Marketing, a coaching business, was born.

This book began as a curriculum outline for my coaching practice. After creating what ultimately became the course outline, I realized that this curriculum was essentially an outline for a book and served as inspiration for me to get writing. As in much of my life, I am not a classically trained marketer or a classically trained writer. I cringe in the direction of the grammar police or word snobs - folks who use grammar as a judgemental weapon. Words to me are like paintbrushes allowing me to use prose, sentences, and phrases to lift, inspire, teach, persuade, and inform.

The marketing scene is dynamic and encompasses a tremendous amount of science and art. It's easy to become overwhelmed by marketing jargon and the numerous techniques, perspectives, and opinions. One can easily fall prey to Doing Without Intention, relying solely upon a few familiar techniques and ignoring the rest. As a marketing generalist, I have an expansive view of marketing, communications, and public relations and appreciate the synergy each provides the other. It's common to find SEO experts, email marketing guides, website designers, marketing communications coaches, and pay-per-click (PPC) advertising advisors, each focused on their small "silo" such that they miss the big picture; however, they will be happy to separate you from your hard-earned money. I'm not saying there isn't a time or place for hiring professionals since that'd be bad for my business. Still, I'm saying that you can benefit from my vast array of marketing experiences to help shape your path forward. As a business owner, you should first be able to do it yourself; once you've mastered the basics, you can continue on the path, train a staff member, or hire a professional.

Consequently, this publication is my do-it-yourself (DIY) guide to marketing, communications, and public relations and is based on my experience, influenced by following my gut, guided in part by the years I've spent as a graduate student and college teacher, and grounded in years of on-the-ground marketing work I've put in.

I put much stock into going with my gut, feeling my intuition, listening to my inner voice, and following that path. Not an approach for everyone, but for me, it's been a journey of discovery filled with interesting people, a wide variety of work experiences, and significant personal growth that led me to write this book. It's been a crazy and enjoyable ride.

I considered naming this book intuitive marketing because I am naturally tuned into my intuitive self. Ultimately, I did come up with another name, as you can see, and throughout this book I'll use the terms holistic and integrative marketing interchangeably. While holistic marketing as a title is appealing, and while I frequently tap into my intuition to help guide my decision-making, it's more than that alone. In medical use, we think of holism as "treating the whole person, taking into account mental and social factors, rather than just the symptoms of an illness." Consequently, I use the term holistic marketing to mean connecting with the whole person, taking into consideration the underlying psychological, behavioral, and emotional factors, understanding the persuasive models of motivation that influence behavior, along with the strategies and tactics of two-way communication, with relationship building at the core.

I am delighted to dedicate this book to the natural healthcare industry, which holds a special place in my heart, and to my wife, Dr. Jill Johnson, ND, a respected member of the natural health community. Her expertise has deeply influenced my perspective. Through her and my interactions with other practitioners, I appreciate their commitment and dedication to their work. In writing this book, I draw from the knowledge and insights gained from these shared experiences. Whether you're a new naturopathic physician, massage therapist, acupuncturist, chiropractor or Reiki healer or someone with years of experience, I hope you find valuable information and inspiration within these pages.

The marketing, communications, and public relations strategies described in this book can be applied to various businesses. Although the examples mainly focus on natural healthcare topics, the information is transferable and valuable for any industry. Additionally, as someone who has spent a significant portion of their career in the wine industry as a marketer, I'll share a few of those experiences to highlight the transferability of the techniques and creativity for your business.

Throughout the book I speak directly to new business owners, but what if you've been doing this work for a while and never took the time to create a marketing plan or brand guide and are still doing well. To you I say congratulations, but if you've picked up this book looking for another perspective, curious about rebranding, or simply want to know more about holistic marketing, that's awesome! Whatever the case, I am glad you're reading and there's so much you can learn by reading this book, and I'd encourage you to read through and take what resonates and grow your business to the next level.

In this book, I guide you from the basics of brand building into the essential concepts of communication, persuasion, and behavioral change, which are critical in ensuring health recommendation compliance. I share the fundamental aspects of creating a striking website; delve into the depths of marketing plans and analysis; spend a good deal of time discussing social media and digital marketing (including sections on PPC, content marketing, email marketing, influencer marketing, and using photography, video, and audio in your marketing. Later in the book, we explore paid advertising, look at traditional and digital advertising, and conclude with a chapter about public relations.

Whether you prefer reading the book cover to cover, jumping around to specific chapters or sections, or using it as a reference tool once you've finished it, the choice is yours. However, as a former college teacher, I recommend reading the book from beginning to end and taking notes (feel free to write directly on the pages). This way, you can refer to specific sections as needed while building your potent marketing program. You've got this and I can't wait to hear about your successes!

As I wrap up this section, I want to pause for a moment and reflect on the circumstances and people who've been helpful to me in the writing of this book. First, to the love of my life, my wife, Dr. Jill Johnson, ND, you've been a great source of inspiration, support, and encouragement and have been a stalwart supporter of my desire to follow my crazy dreams wherever they take us. Thank you for giving me the space I needed to find myself again, and in the process, I've regained my love of writing and passion for learning.

I also want to thank my adult children and their significant others (Logan and his family, Kelly-Rae, Wilder & River, and dogs, Coffee and Jasper, and my youngest son, Tyler and Brittany), who've been supportive, encouraging, and interested in hearing about this book and my coaching business.

To my current and former clients, I am grateful for allowing me into your life and letting me help your business grow; in doing so, providing me with space to mature in my role as a coach. You're fantastic, and I am grateful. To my former employers: thanks for the opportunities to learn and grow, to share my knowledge, and to help grow your business; and to the one who "let me go," - thank you!

I'd be remiss if I didn't give acknowledgement to the City of Kenmore, WA - The Hanger, a public space and coffee shop where I wrote this book, every weekday morning from 8:30 am to 12:00 pm. Public spaces are incredibly valuable to writers, freelancers, consultants, and officeless folks to create art, do business, and meet socially. The Hanger should be a model for every community, nice job and thank you!

Finally, I'd like to say thank you to the natural medicine community for hanging in there as conventional medicine, skeptics, naysayers, and pharmaceutical industry opponents push back against the tide of traditional medicine. Natural medicine modalities, herbal preparations, acupuncture, physical and spiritual medicine, and personal connection is the cure for what ails us. And while conventional medicine has its place, there is no replacing time-tested natural medicine practices in healing the mind, body, and spirit. Keep on keeping on!

BUILDING A BRAND THAT LASTS:
Essential Elements of Brand Identity

"Your brand is the single most important investment you can make in your business."

- Steve Forbes

Think of a brand you're familiar with, and most likely, your mind will drift to one of the biggies, such as Nike, McDonald's, or Coca Cola, for example. Each of these companies will probably elicit an emotional response from you when you read their names, and you probably have an opinion about them, too, whether or not you are or have been their customer. Big business spends a tremendous amount of time and financial resources to create their brand, protect their brand, and shape how we view their brand. And, as small business owners, we need to do the same.

In his 2005 book, The Brand Gap, author Marty Neumeier states "A brand is not a logo. A brand is not a corporate identity system. It's a person's gut feeling about a product, service, or company. Because it depends on others for its existence, it must become a guarantee of trustworthy behavior. Good branding makes business integral to society and creates opportunity for everyone, from the chief executive to the most distant customer."

Hold on for a moment. In other words, companies spend a fortune to create a brand and protect a brand in the hopes that we, the consumers, agree with how they present themselves.

Kind of!

As a business, we initially forge our business's identity or personality by establishing our mission statement, which serves as our guiding principle of how we will conduct ourselves. Next, we create the voice or tone for our organization (e.g., friendly, warm, kind, professional, cutting-edge, traditional, clinical, etc.). We communicate with our prospective and current clients/patients using this tone. The brand, therefore, becomes a co-creation between our business and our clients' perception of us. When both are in alignment, we're on the right path - and our brand is strengthened.

Brand Tip - Your Brand is a Co-Creation Between Your Business and Clients

In addition to the guiding principles of our mission statement expressed through our voice, we also need to create a visual identity in the form of logos, style, and fonts. Consistently using these elements in our communications and marketing reinforces how we are perceived and enhances our brand presence in the marketplace.

A natural health practice can build its brand by creating a mission statement that reflects its values and goals, such as providing high-quality, client/patient-centered care. They can also create a professional and approachable logo and visual identity and establish a consistent message and tone across their website, social media, advertising, and patient interactions.

One example of a well-known conventional medical practice that has built a strong brand is the Mayo Clinic. The Mayo Clinic has a clear mission statement, "To inspire hope and contribute to health and well-being by providing the best care to every patient through integrated clinical practice, education, and research," a recognizable logo and a consistent message and tone across all communication channels. Additionally, Mayo Clinic is known to be a pioneer in the medical field, and its brand is associated with the highest level of medical expertise and patient care.

For many of the early pioneering businesses their brand emerged as a consequence of marketing, only later to be systematically organized into a guide that keeps everyone in the organization on the same page - this document became known as a Brand Guide or Brand Book.

Before We Build a Brand Guide

"A brand guide is the foundation for a consistent brand experience. It's the roadmap for how to communicate your brand visually and verbally." - Neil Patel

It's important to remember the contents of this book are intended to help you grow your business. Ultimately all the hard work you're doing will pay off with your ideal customers, clients or patients finding your business, increased appointments, sales and growth. By establishing your brand guide (and your associated planning documents) early in the development of your business you'll be setting the tone, reducing the downstream headaches that procrastination brings, and establishing yourself and your business as an industry leader.

So, all of this is to say, these are your documents and they need to serve you. If you'd like to create a 10 page brand guide, go for it; however, if you'd like something more concise, then create a 1-pager. The point is whatever planning documents you create need to fit your style with an eye to the future if/when you bring on additional staff, a new office, start purchasing advertisements you'll be glad you did. In the long term you'll benefit from this process as long as you follow the recommendations within this book.

It's worth the effort it takes to create a Brand Guide because it forces you to consider and process core mission and branding materials, plus it can be a lot of fun! First, I'll guide you through the essential individual elements of a Brand Guide, then afterwards, I'll share a template you can use. Here goes!

Design Considerations

Before I delve into the specific elements within your Brand Guide and since you're about to embark upon a design process it's a good idea to think ahead to how you might use the graphics.

This is important: prior to launching into a design project you'll want to determine and anticipate the various ways you may use your designs. For example, if you're going to want to have a sign printed from a local or national printer you'll need to have the designs saved as a particular file type (e.g., Vector files, such as AI, EPS, PDF or SVG file extensions). If all of this sounds confusing, that's okay, having one of these types of files on hand will help you immensely as you speak to your printer. Unless you're familiar with graphic design programs, such as Adobe products, you'll want to have someone on your team to help you out. For example, if you try to create a door sign or an outdoor A-Frame sign and you only have a JPEG file you'll run into quality issues related to resolution - it's frustrating and costly to have a large sign printed that is blurry (more about that in a bit).

Examples of Fundamental File Extension Types:

- <u>JPEG</u> - JPEG (named for and created by the Joint Photographic Experts Group) tends to be a smaller sized file and because of its size it's handy for use on webpages allowing for quicker load times.

- <u>PNG</u> - The PNG (Portable Network Graphic) is a larger type of file that allows for transparent backgrounds and is ideal for graphic design. I use PNG for most of my design work for social media.

- <u>PDF</u> - PDF's (Portable Document Format) is an easily shareable document type.

- <u>Vector files</u> - Vector format is useful when wanting a high resolution image that is scalable without distortion. Examples of vector files are AI (Adobe Illustrator), EPS (Encapsulated PostScript), SVG (Scalable Vector Graphics), and PDF (Portable Document Format).

Color Space

Color space refers to the capacity of an output device (e.g., printed document or image, digital representation, or electronic device) to display the color. Below is a listing of the primary color spaces I've used for digital and print work over the years, they include:

- <u>RGB</u> - RGB is shorthand for Red, Green, Blue and is used to display the color spectrum for digital devices and photos on computer screens and televisions.

- <u>Hex</u> - The Hex is a color system often used in website and graphic design. The Hex system uses a hexadecimal code, made up of three pairs of characters each representing color values of Red, Green and Blue (RGB). Each color has a number (from 0 to 255) with each color code broken down into 2 hexadecimal numbers. For example, the color white is displayed as #FFFFFF and black as #000000.

- <u>CMYK</u> - CMYK is used in the printing profession for printing newspapers and magazines. The CMYK represents the four colors that make up the primary color scheme (i.e., Cyan, Magenta, Yellow, Black).

- <u>Pantone</u> - To ensure accuracy and consistency in print color reproduction the Pantone system was created to standardize color matching.

As an important part of your Brand Guide, include each of your brand colors along with their individual codes for each of the color spaces: RGB, HEX, and CMYK.

Let's consider a couple of illustrative examples combining file extension and color space concepts and the importance of choice. Project 1 Example: we want to create a social media marketing campaign about the importance of having an annual health screening. You authored the written content, selected an attractive JPEG image, and are working in the RGB color space. Then, you choose to use your handy online graphic design program, such as Canva, to create your design. Afterwards, you review it and it looks good on your computer, and decide to use this content for both a blog posting and for a social media post (we'll talk more about Content Marketing later on). After posting, you view the content on your mobile device and it looks great, and your blog looks nice too, plus the image loads quickly because of the small file size. Enjoy the win!

Project 2 Example: the initial Project 1 campaign went very well, so well in fact, that you've decided to have an A-Frame sign printed by your local printer and to place it outside of your office so potential clients can see it as they pass. You send those same graphics (JPEG/ RGB) to the printer with the specifications (the dimensions and quantity we want printed) and when you pick up the finished product you are immediately disappointed. Why? The image looks terrible because the graphics are not scalable (non-vector file) so when the printer enlarged the image it distorted badly and became blurry; additionally, because you used the RGB color space the colors look muted. The digital version in comparison looked great. What could you have done differently? If instead, you had created this to-be-printed version using a scalable design (e.g., Vector File - AI, EPS, PDF, etc.) the printer could have enlarged the image without distortion; additionally, if you had chosen the CMYK color space, the color space in which most printers use, then the colors would have been more true, vibrant and not muddy. The sign would have been attractive, clients would take notice and you'd be pleased for making a good decision early in the design process, and saved time and money from having to remake the design.

This is only one of the reasons why it's so important to think ahead and imagine all of the possible uses for the graphic designs you're creating. Additionally, building a positive working relationship with your printer will be helpful. The Brand Guide building process will help you develop a killer brand and once it's done, it's set and it serves to keep your branding consistent, attractive and memorable.

Let's Build A Brand Guide

> *"Your brand guide is your secret weapon for creating a consistent, memorable brand experience." - Tara Gentile*

The first step in creating a memorable brand requires you to thoughtfully work through the brand building process. A brand guide is a document that describes the visual and verbal elements that make up your businesses' brand. Keep in mind, a brand is a co-creation between you and your customers. As I will repeat frequently throughout this book, all of the planning documents are intended to serve an internal audience, you and your team, therefore create your documents in a manner that makes them easy to create and simple to use. The elements of a brand guide often include:

1. Logo - A unique symbol that represents your brand.
2. Typography - The typefaces used in written materials.

3. Color Palette - The colors used in the brand's visual materials.
4. Imagery - The visual style of photos and illustrations used in your brand's materials.
5. The Tone of Voice - The language style used in written communications.
6. Tagline - A short phrase that describes your brand message.
7. Brand Story - The background, history, and personality of your brand.

Here's a fun-to-know fact, the term "brand" originated from the Old Norse word "brandr" meaning "to burn." In ancient times and still today, cattle owners would burn their marks onto the animals to indicate ownership. Throughout history, the brand became known as any distinctive mark or symbol used to identify a particular product or manufacturer.

Logo

Marketing folks began using branding as a marketing tool in the early 20th century. Big companies began using brand names and logos to serve as a way to differentiate themselves from their competitors.

A lot of folks think of a business logo as being synonymous with a brand. While it may seem confusing, a logo is a part of a brand but is not, by itself, a brand. Although the notion of a brand has changed since the old times, it still serves as a visual representation of ownership.

A logo is crucial because it visualizes a brand and helps establish recognition and differentiation. A well-designed logo can also convey a brand's personality and values. Creating a logo typically involves researching the brand and its target audience, developing concept ideas, and refining and finalizing the chosen design. This process may involve working with a graphic designer or design team. It may also include testing the logo with a focus group or other target audience to ensure it effectively communicates the desired message.

While I am fond of saying all business owners ought to be able to do every aspect of their businesses themselves, there are occasions when hiring a specialist will come in handy, and creating a logo may be one of those times. In our own businesses, we've engaged professional designers, sought help from knowledgeable friends, and made our own. First, a word of caution: while our friends may have incredible talent and skill, there are pitfalls to soliciting their help. For example, what happens if, after several attempts, you still don't like their design? What if they get upset? What if they take longer than you'd like? What if their feelings get hurt? For these reasons alone, it may be best to seek outside help. Here are some ways you can bring your designs to life:

- <u>DIY</u> - With the growing number of online design programs, it can be a fun way to Do It Yourself (DIY). Without delving too deeply into the number of online programs you can use, since they come and go rather quickly, I'll point to a couple of my favorites.

  ○ Canva - this online design program has free and paid subscriptions allowing you to design and save documents in a variety of formats (more about formats later). Visit: www.canva.com[1]

  ○ Adobe Express (formerly Spark) - This is a "free online and mobile graphic design app used to create images, videos and web pages" (Adobe). Visit: https://www.adobe.com/express/

- <u>Hire a Professional Designer</u> - Hiring someone who understands logos and brand guide development can

---

1. http://www.canva.com

simplify the entire process; however, the costs can quickly become prohibitively expensive.

○ Local Marketing Agency - The local marketing agency knows the ins and outs of brand guide development and, after a meeting or two, can create several iterations of a logo for you.

○ Local Independent Designer - Hiring a local graphic designer can be an excellent alternative to working with a marketing agency. It will be much less expensive.

○ Online Independent Designer - We've enjoyed working with independent online designers from websites that have popped up over the past several years. When we created Blue Earth Medicine, we reached out to 99Designs with our logo needs, shared our desires and basic color preferences, set a budget, and began. We rated the initial designs, asked for a few modifications, and nailed down an attractive design from a designer in Peru. We still love the design. Here are a few of our favorite online design platforms (but there are many more):

- 99Designs - https://99designs.com/

- Design Crowd - https://www.designcrowd.com/

- Fiverr - https://www.fiverr.com

Building a successful practice or business takes time, financial resources and patience. You may have all three or might be lacking in one, perhaps the financial resources. No doubt this makes launching a business a bit more tricky, but you've got this and with this book and with my free Marketing Plan guide (available at www.bradjohnsonmarketing.com) you can do it yourself. It's okay if your first attempts are created by yourself or a friend, it's more important to move forward than to be frozen because you can't afford a professional designer or consultant. I often think of the aphorism, "perfect is the enemy of good" (commonly attributed to Voltaire) when I'm feeling a little stuck. I'm fond of saying this to my clients: "don't let perfection get in the way of progress."

Business & Life Tip: Don't Let Perfection Get in the Way of Progress

Typography/Font usage

As you're probably gathering by now, having consistency is the name of the branding game, and we're taking a deep dive into this section as we work our way through. Remember, nothing about marketing, branding, advertising, public relations, and communication is life or death. However, it does work in our best interest when we're trying to build a brand, to play the long game, and have as good a road map as possible so our work life is more streamlined as our business grows. Planning and dealing with these details within the brand guide will make your daily work life smoother and more predictable. For example, a brand guide's typeface or font section typically includes information about the specific typefaces you approve for official communications and materials for a particular brand. In addition, the guide can include information about the style of the typeface (such as whether it is serif or sans-serif), the specific variations of the typeface (such as bold or italic), and any guidelines for using the typeface (such as size and spacing requirements).

For example, a brand guide for a Yoga studio might specify that the official typeface is "Open Sans" and to be used in all official communications and materials. The guide might also set usage for regular, bold, and italic variations of the typeface and that the font size should be no smaller than 12 points. Additionally, the brand guide may specify that another typeface, such as "Lato," should be used for headlines and that all headlines should be bold.

Color Palette

The colors you choose for your brand send an important message to your customers, patients, and clients, conveying subtle messages about your business. A color palette is an essential element of a brand guide because it helps create a consistent visual identity. The colors used in a brand's marketing materials, such as its logo, website, and packaging, should be consistent across all platforms to create a cohesive and recognizable brand.

IKEA does a great job of conveying its brand through color with its iconic blue and yellow color scheme. The colors are easily recognizable and are associated with the brand, making it easy for customers to identify IKEA products in a store or online. Conversely, when a brand frequently changes its colors or when the colors need to be better coordinated, it can appear unprofessional or may not be as effective in attracting customers. Inconsistency in brand content can be confusing for customers. It can make it difficult for the brand to establish a solid visual identity.

The color palette section of a brand guide typically includes information about the specific colors approved for use in official communications and materials for a particular brand. This can consist of information about the specific Hex codes or RGB/CMYK values of the colors, as well as any guidelines for how the colors should be used (such as which colors should be used as background colors and which colors should be used for text and imagery).

For example, a brand guide for a tech company might specify that the official colors are blue (#0077C9), black (#000000), and white (#FFFFFF) and that these colors should be used in all official communications and materials. The guide might also specify that blue should be used as the primary color, black should be used for text, and white should be used as a background color. Additionally, the brand guide may specify different shades of blue for other use cases.

It also shows how these colors should be used with other design elements such as typography, imagery, and layout, such as:

- The percentage of color usage to imagery, background, typography

- How the colors should be used in different mediums such as digital, print, packaging, and other applications

- Color contrast and accessibility guidelines for people with visual impairment.

The point I'm making with these brand guide elements is that it's essential to consider how you want your business to be perceived. Through thoughtful planning, you'll have the foundation for your business established, making each subsequent step less burdensome, more streamlined, and ultimately making doing business easier. This is your business, and you can go as deep into any of these practices as you'd like. Keep your brand guide clear, concise, and easy to use.

Imagery

Imagery refers to the stylistic elements of your brand. It includes visual components of photography, video, graphics, and illustrations used in your brand materials. Leaning into your color palette as a reference will help shape the visual appeal of your brand.

Tone of Voice

Stylistically the tone of voice of your brand is how your messaging comes off in written communications. Your brand guide refers to the specific style or personality your business or practice wants to convey to your target market through its messaging. In effect, the tone of voice is how a company wants its messaging to be perceived by the target audience, choice of language, style, and overall feel.

Here are several interrelated tone of voice examples that a natural health practitioner may choose to include in their brand guide:

- Warm and empathetic

- Trustworthy and knowledgeable

- Inspiring, and uplifting

Putting these stylistic elements into action, we could imagine a natural healthcare provider to have a "tone of voice" in their messaging: "At Tall Pines Natural Medicine, we believe in treating our patients with care and compassion. Our goal is to empower individuals to take control of their well-being through holistic, natural solutions. Therefore, we approach every consultation with a positive, solutions-focused attitude, striving to educate and inspire our patients on their journey to optimal health."

Tagline

A tagline is a short phrase that summarizes the essence of a brand and its message. In a brand guide, the tagline serves as a memorable and concise representation of the brand's personality, values, and purpose. It helps to reinforce the brand's identity and differentiate it from competitors. Similarly, in advertising, the term "slogan" is used for specific campaigns or promotions to generate interest with a shorter-term phrase.

For example, a tagline for a natural healthcare practice could be "Nurture your well-being naturally." This tagline emphasizes the brand's commitment to using natural and holistic approaches to healthcare and positions the brand as a trusted and caring provider of health services.

Brand Story

A brand story chronicles and communicates a brand's history, values, mission, and personality. It serves as the backbone for a brand's identity and helps to establish an emotional connection with customers. Let's look at a fictitious natural health business - "Natura."

Brand Story: Natura is a natural health business founded to empower individuals to lead healthier, more fulfilling lives. Our founder, a passionate herbalist and wellness expert, discovered natural remedies' power in her wellness journey. Frustrated by the limited options, she created a space where individuals could access high-quality natural remedies and expert guidance. Today, Natura continues to be a leader in the natural health community, offering a range of products and services to support individuals on their wellness journeys.

Our brand is built on three core values: authenticity, empowerment, and community. We trust in the power of nature to heal and are committed to providing only the highest quality natural remedies. Our team of expert practitioners is dedicated to empowering individuals with the knowledge and tools they need to take control of their health. And we believe in the importance of community, offering regular workshops and events to bring people together and share their experiences and knowledge.

At Natura, we are more than just a business - we're a community of individuals passionate about wellness. So join us on our journey to better health, naturally.

Brand Guide

Remember, a brand guide is a document that outlines the specific visual and written elements that make up your brand. This is more than a creative exercise. Establishing a brand guide is a foundational step in creating what your brand will look like, sound like, and at the end of the day, what we hope our clients believe to be true about our business. Earlier, I pointed out that your brand guide is for you, your employees, or contractors to rely on to ensure your brand is consistent, attractive, and appropriately represents your business and practice.

Here is an example of a simple brand guide from Blue Earth Medicine, my wife's naturopathic medical practice:

- Brand Name: Blue Earth Medicine

- Logo: A stylized representation of hands, leaf, and earth.

- Color Palette: Shades of blue and natural earth tones.

- Typography: A clean, bold Raleway font for headings and a Raleway regular font for body text.

- Imagery: Photos of Dr. Jill, natural environments, and illustrations of plants and herbs.

- The tone of Voice: Trustworthy, knowledgeable, approachable, and holistic.

- Tagline: "Live Better with Naturopathic Care."

Brand Story: Blue Earth Medicine is a naturopathic medical practice focusing on family medicine, chronic illness, hormone imbalances, and cognitive decline using nature-based plant medicines, hydrotherapy, homeopathy, and other natural modalities. Our mission is to promote wellness through time-tested naturopathic medicine and holistic and personalized care while educating the community on the benefits of natural healing.

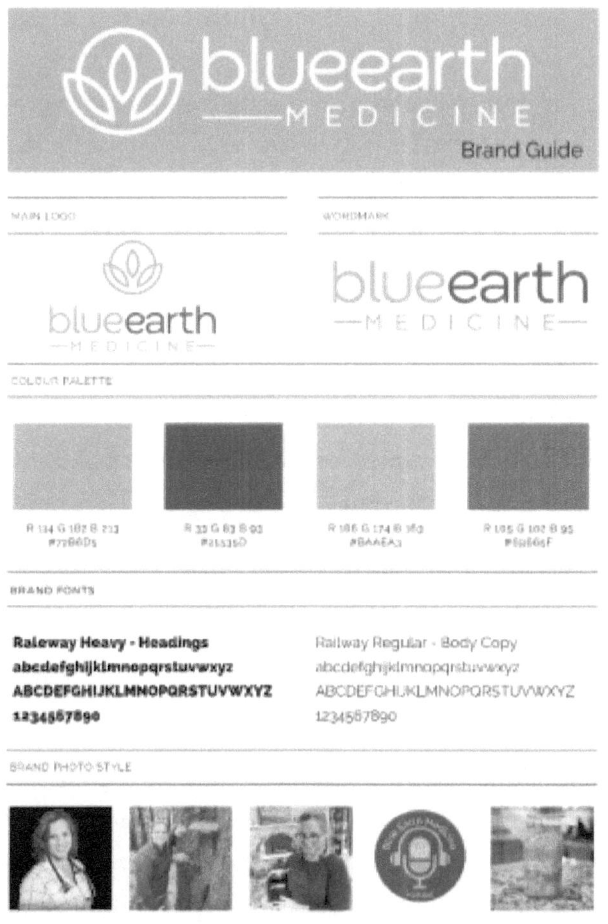

Final Thoughts

Be realistic, be authentic, and make sure to follow your plans. I once worked for a company that spent thousands of dollars with a marketing firm to create a brand guide, marketing materials, website, and print materials throwing in all the bells and whistles. The brand guide they made was beautiful and comprehensive. Unfortunately, despite the time and money that went into creating those materials, most of the management team wasn't aware of their existence. Therefore, much of the advice I give my clients and you in this book is to be authentic, realistic and follow your plans. Suppose you're planning to be a solo practitioner or want to build a corporate empire, more power to you! I want you to do business wisely, with forethought and an eye toward the future. Taking your precious time to create a brand guide (and, later in this book, a marketing plan) is essential to creating a successful, thriving, and prosperous business. It's only a frivolous exercise if you spend the time to develop these important documents and then ignore them.

Even if you're familiar with putting a business or natural health practice together, you may be tempted to skip the brand guide step or forgo creating a marketing plan, but I'd argue that'd be a mistake. As in your professional education, having a firm foundation established from the outset will lay the groundwork for everything that comes later. By committing to the success of your business/practice from the beginning by taking the necessary time to contemplate and develop a brand guide, you'll soon be on a path to prosperity.

Your brand guide sets the tone for everything that comes afterward; it represents the personality of your business/practice and is ultimately how we want to be seen, so take the time, do it today, start right now, put this book down, and get to it! If you already have some (or all) of the elements, great; if not, that's fine - You've Got This!

Did you put the book down and start yet?

WINNING HEARTS & MINDS:

The Science of Communication & Persuasion

"Behavioral and persuasive theory provides a scientific basis for understanding how people make decisions and what motivates them to change their behavior. Businesses and medical practitioners who understand these principles can more effectively communicate with their audiences and achieve their goals."

- Shelley E. Taylor

Before we leap into the wild world of marketing, I feel it's essential to get a good grip on communication style and what we mean by good communication, and then delve into the fascinating subject of influence and persuasion, one of my favorite subjects. After all, as a natural healthcare practitioner (or accountant), one of the most critical skills you need to foster is clearly and effectively communicating with your clients and customers and ensuring they follow your advice - that's where the power of influence comes in.

First, we'll explore the topic of communication style. Communication style refers to the way people communicate and interact with others. It encompasses verbal and nonverbal communication, including tone of voice, body language, word choice, and pacing. Communication style can significantly impact how well individuals can express themselves, convey information, and build relationships with others.

Let's also keep in mind the four types of workplace communication, some overlap with the above list:

● Verbal communication

- Non-verbal communication (body language and facial expressions)

- Phone Communication

- Written communication (e.g., letters, documents, emails, and text messages)

To understand your communication style, you can use a tool such as the Communication Styles Assessment - I've included a link to a basic style test below. This assessment is designed to help individuals identify their dominant communication style based on four categories: assertive, aggressive, passive, and passive-aggressive.

An assertive communication style involves expressing oneself directly and honestly while also respecting the needs and opinions of others. On the other hand, an aggressive communication style consists of speaking in a forceful and confrontational way, often disregarding the feelings and thoughts of others. A passive communication style involves avoiding conflict and asserting oneself, often leading to difficulty in expressing one's own needs and desires. Lastly, a passive-aggressive communication style consists of expressing anger or frustration subtly or indirectly, often leading to confusion and misunderstandings.

By taking the Communication Styles Assessment, individuals can gain insight into their communication tendencies and identify areas where they may want to improve their communication skills. With this knowledge, individuals can communicate more effectively and build stronger relationships with others.

To test your basic communication style, visit: https://communication-styles.com/

What Makes for Good Conversation?

Think back to when you had a good conversation with a friend, colleague, mentor, or loved one, and then take a moment to consider what made it a "good conversation." (I'll wait while you think about this). What about the conversation that made it "good," and how did that particular conversation differ from other ordinary conversations that were less than good? Communication researchers have identified six critical components of a good conversation: active listening, mutual respect, open-mindedness, clear communication, empathy, and authenticity. Let's take a look at what each of the six components tells us:

Active Listening: Effective communication hinges on the fundamental practice of active listening, wherein one pays close attention to the words spoken by the other person and responds thoughtfully. Peter Drucker, a renowned management consultant, and author, emphasizes that active listening surpasses mere verbal communication, extending to discerning the unspoken messages conveyed by the speaker. By attentively considering the other person's words and providing thoughtful responses, we demonstrate our commitment to avoiding interruptions and speaking over them, fostering meaningful dialogue.

"The most important thing in communication is hearing what isn't said."
- Peter Drucker

Mutual Respect: Respectful communication forms the cornerstone of a meaningful conversation. Each participant needs to recognize and appreciate the opinions of others, even in cases of disagreement. Hence, mutual respect lays the foundation for productive dialogues. However, it's important to note that valuing someone's opinion does not necessitate complete agreement. It simply signifies a willingness to recognize and honor the perspectives put forth by others.

"Respect is how to treat everyone, not just those you want to impress." - Richard Branson

<u>Open-Mindedness</u>: Embracing an open-minded attitude entails a willingness to explore fresh ideas and diverse perspectives. Engaging in a meaningful conversation necessitates a receptive mindset that embraces the opportunity to learn from others while remaining prepared to challenge personal assumptions. By cultivating an open mind, one can reap the abundant benefits of welcoming new concepts, alternative viewpoints, and innovative insights during conversations. Keeping the door ajar to novel ideas, perspectives, and advancements enriches the exchange and fosters intellectual growth.

"In a world that is constantly changing, there is no one subject or set of subjects that will serve you for the foreseeable future, let alone for the rest of your life. The most important skill to acquire now is learning how to learn."

- Naisbitt

<u>Clear Communication</u>: While some individuals possess a natural aptitude for clear communication, others, like myself, may encounter challenges expressing themselves verbally and find solace in written communication. Interestingly, both groups often admire the strengths of the other. Consequently, ensuring clear and concise communication is the key to fostering effective conversations. It is crucial to express intentions with clarity and deliver messages in a manner that is easily comprehensible to others. To achieve this, periodic check-ins become paramount. One can ascertain if the intended message is being conveyed accurately by seeking confirmation from the listener. This can be accomplished by asking if the other person understands or requesting them to summarize the shared information. Such practices enable a more comprehensive understanding of whether one's message has been successfully received and comprehended by the listener.

"The single biggest problem in communication is the illusion that it has taken place."

- George Bernard Shaw

<u>Empathy</u>: The practice of empathy plays a vital role in our ability to comprehend and empathize with others' emotions and messages. By actively engaging in empathy, we foster trust and facilitate meaningful conversations. In addition, empathy serves as a cornerstone for building connections and enables us to delve into a deeper level of understanding, appreciating diverse perspectives. In essence, empathy acts as a catalyst, allowing individuals to forge a profound connection and truly grasp the experiences and viewpoints of others.

"When you show deep empathy toward others, their defensive energy goes down, and positive energy replaces it. That's when you can get more creative in solving problems."

- Stephen Covey

<u>Authenticity</u>: This is one of those things that when you feel it, you know it. In an authentic conversation, thoughts, emotions, and intentions are expressed sincerely. When participants engage authentically, they allow their true selves to be seen, fostering an environment of openness and vulnerability. This transparency cultivates trust as others perceive the absence of pretense or hidden agendas.

Authenticity transcends mere surface-level interactions, encouraging more profound and genuine exchanges. When individuals are authentic, they invite others to reciprocate, establishing a safe space for honest and meaningful dialogue. This real connection fosters a greater understanding and appreciation for each other's perspectives, enhancing the overall quality and depth of the conversation.

"Authenticity is the alignment of head, mouth, heart, and feet – thinking, saying, feeling, and doing the same thing – consistently. This builds trust, and followers love leaders they can trust." - Lance Secretan

When we apply these communication principles to our everyday life and professional endeavors, our conversations will be more engaging, relevant, enlightening, and fulfilling. A good conversation is a two-way exchange that involves active listening, mutual respect, open-mindedness, clear communication, empathy, and authenticity. Therefore, please monitor your communications and reflect deeply upon whether you communicate in a way that includes these six principles. If not, I'd challenge you to incorporate these teachings into your everyday communications and business practices.

But what good are all of our plans if our clients don't show up for their appointments and we're left with an empty exam room? That's lost revenue and frustration. Getting clients and patients to show up for appointments, follow directions and comply with your recommendations is paramount to ensuring healing occurs. Fortunately, social scientists have taken up this vital mission. We now have a deeper understanding of how people make decisions and why they do what they do. We have discovered approaches that help ensure compliance through persuasive techniques.

Next, we turn our attention to how people process information and then begin a discussion on the foundations of behavior and methods of persuasion.

The Psychology of Behavior and Persuasion

Owning a business can be frustrating. Whether you own a medical practice or an automotive service station, when a client fails to show up for their appointment that it begins to wear on a business owner. Medical doctors (MDs) long ago moved away from a medical care model to a business model, and it shows. No doubt you've made an appointment with a busy practice, arrived on time, sat for 20 minutes in a crowded lobby with a dozen sick people waiting, then were escorted to an exam room where you sat alone staring at barren walls, then waited another 20 minutes for the doctor to make a brief appearance only to vanish moments later. Many of us, while waiting, wonder, "what in the world is going on?" as we count the ceiling tiles. Aside from the insurance company's robust control over physicians, most conventional medical facilities rely on the business model to make their fortunes.

Fortunately, it's been almost a decade since I spent time waiting for a doctor to see me in one of those small, sterile rooms. I remember one doctor I knew had four patient rooms running simultaneously. His nurses would bring patients into the inner medical office, weigh and measure, take the initial medical assessment, and pass off the information to the doctor, who'd later arrive and have a diagnosis - even before meeting with the patient. Wow, talk about efficiency! The conventional medicine model is a profitable business model but needs to be improved as a patient-centered medical model.

The truth is, I get it. But, business model aside, most of us understand how frustrating it is to have set up an appointment only to be forgotten by a service provider. It's infuriating, especially if you've been looking forward to the appointment for a long time. But conversely, my wife, a naturopathic doctor, experiences the same frustration when patients neglect to cancel their visits ahead of time. Because she is a patient-centered practice, she blocks out 60 minutes for each patient, and when someone fails to show, it's more than frustrating; it's a loss of income.

So, how can a practice enhance patient compliance and appointment-keeping? The noted social psychologist professor and author Robert B. Cialdini, in his highly regarded book "Influence:

Science and Practice," showcases dozens of approaches he researched and tested out while posing as a salesperson in several industries, and I'll distill several of his recommendations into valuable methods you can apply today. Let's go!

Thinking on Auto-Pilot

Cialdini starts off his book by suggesting much of our cognition (i.e., thoughts, memories, recollections) is on autopilot, and surprisingly happening without much active awareness. Humans respond with the same sort of automaticity and quick responses as seen in wildlife, called fixed pattern behaviors. This is interesting: in a 1978 study, three social psychology scientists (Langer, Blanc & Chanowitz) studied automaticity in human behavior by setting up a simple experiment. They investigated the commonly held understanding that people are more likely to do a favor if the asker has a reason for the favor. People asking for a small favor, with a reason, were overwhelmingly more likely to jump ahead in the photocopy line, ahead of those without a stated reason - 94% vs. 60%! But, get this, the reason given didn't seem to matter. Check out the differences:

1. "Excuse me, I have five pages. May I use the Xerox machine?"
2. "Excuse me, I have five pages. May I use the Xerox machine because I'm in a rush?"

Interestingly, they still achieved a 60% success rate in the condition without a specific reason - just by asking. However, in the situation where the student applied a justification, the reason for the favor, they were much more successful in jumping ahead in the line. So, the researchers wondered if the favor was due to the fact that someone had a specific reason or if it was due to the word "because," so they tested that out.

1. "Excuse me, I have five pages. May I use the Xerox machine because I need to make some copies?"

Like the initial findings, the "because" trigger resulted in a 93% success rate. While the study authors do not believe this automaticity works in every situation, the fact that it works on many occasions makes it worth keeping in mind.

For example, researchers found automaticity to be fully present in a similar study. The research highlights the importance and potential pitfalls of mental shortcuts, called heuristics. The authors cite a case where well-off travelers to Arizona went shopping for jewelry and, with little knowledge of turquoise, applied a stereotype heuristic, expensive = good, to their purchase behaviors. Without the necessary knowledge of a product or service, we rely on mental shortcuts to help us process vast amounts of information. We often see this same thing in car or clothing purchases; if it costs more, it must be better. While an expeditious way to process information, relying too firmly on heuristics can also land you with a drawer full of "junk" jewelry.

Since we'll spend several pages discussing influence and persuasion, I want to pause to discuss the importance of being ethical in business dealings. You see, while much of the information I'll provide is commonly known, there've been some bad apples who've used this knowledge for darker purposes over time. I know you never would, but I'll feel better by saying this: be decent, be kind, and use this information for good - to help your patients and clients achieve the goals they have set. Okay, the lecture is done.

Because I mentioned heuristics, I'd like to review this concept more, expanding on the benefits and drawbacks. This knowledge will benefit your personal and professional growth; having insights into why our clients behave in the ways they do will be of great value to your business. So let's explore mental shortcuts.

Mental Shortcuts

Heuristics are essentially "rules of thumb" or mental shortcuts that people use to make decisions quickly and efficiently. They are strategies that people use when they need complete information or when they need to make a decision quickly. In the healthcare industry, heuristics can be used to guide decision-making in natural medicine. Mental shortcuts serve the purpose of minimizing one's cognitive load and boosting efficiency in mental processing. But, there is also a cost to this type of top-down processing which relies on personal experiences and shared experiences of those around you (bottom-up processing uses a systematic process of using sensory information starting from the most basic features and building up to a more complex understanding). As a healthcare professional, it's good to know your knowledge and experience can come together and provide quick answers to sometimes complicated cases; however, when we overly rely on heuristics, we may be doing more harm than good. Additionally, mental shortcuts can result in lazy thinking, stereotypes being a good example, with long-term and damaging consequences.

Recognizing that we rely heavily on heuristics to reduce our cognitive load, we need to stay vigilant, not underthink, and apply constructive thought processes instead. Of course, this goes for the practitioner and the patient, as everyone relies on mental shortcuts to minimize deliberative thinking and make everyday living easier.

Mental shortcuts are crucial in our decision-making process. These cognitive strategies enable us to assess and judge various situations and information we encounter quickly. Several types of heuristics help simplify complex problems and assist us in navigating the complexities of daily life. There are several types of heuristics:

<u>Availability heuristic</u>: This heuristic involves making decisions based on the most readily available information that comes to mind quickly. For

example, a natural medicine practitioner might recommend Echinacea for a cold because they have had several patients who reported feeling better after taking it. On the other hand, a patient may use the availability heuristic if they have heard a lot about the benefits of taking Turmeric for inflammation; they may be more likely to choose Turmeric supplements over other options. Just because a solution to a problem comes to mind quickly does not mean it's the best option. So, when an answer seems obvious, pause and consider other options.

<u>Representativeness heuristic</u>: This heuristic involves making decisions based on how well something matches a particular prototype or stereotype. For example, a practitioner might assume that a patient with a specific set of symptoms has a condition because those symptoms are typical of that condition (i.e., a patient with a fever and a sore throat has strep throat because those are common symptoms of that condition.).On the other hand, a patient may apply the representativeness heuristic by believing natural remedies are always safe and effective; therefore, they may be more likely to choose a natural supplement over a synthetic one.

<u>Anchoring and adjustment heuristic</u>: This heuristic involves making decisions based on an initial value (or anchor) and then adjusting that value based on additional information. For example, a natural medicine practitioner might recommend a particular dosage of a natural supplement based on the recommended dosage on the label but then adjust that dosage based on the patient's age, weight, and other factors. Likewise, a patient may read that a particular supplement is effective in a small study and may anchor on that information and adjust their decision based on the size and quality of the study.

<u>Confirmation bias</u>: This heuristic involves seeking information confirming our preexisting beliefs or hypotheses and ignoring information that contradicts them. In other words, we seek

information confirming our opinion about something. In our everyday lives, we see people choosing news outlets to pander to their beliefs, often at the expense of truth. In healthcare, for example, a natural medicine practitioner might only read studies that support the use of a particular herb for a specific condition and ignore studies suggesting that the herb is ineffective for that condition. Scientific rigor requires an open mind, a truly open mind able to consider many options. Similarly, patients may believe that a particular supplement is effective and may only seek out positive reviews and ignore negative ones.

<u>Hindsight bias</u>: This is the "I knew it all along" heuristic. This heuristic involves believing that an event is more predictable than it was after it occurred. For example, a natural medicine practitioner might think that they knew all along that a particular natural medicine treatment would be effective for a patient's condition, even though they were unsure when they made the recommendation. On the other hand, suppose a patient starts taking a natural supplement or remedy for a particular health condition and experiences a positive outcome. In that case, hindsight bias can lead them to believe that they always knew the supplement or remedy would work, even if they had initially been skeptical or had no prior experience with it. This bias can be dangerous, especially when making health-related decisions. It can cause people to overlook the potential risks or downsides of a particular supplement or remedy and rely too heavily on their own perceived expertise or intuition.

It's important for natural medicine practitioners to be aware of these kinds of mental shortcuts and try to avoid relying on them too heavily. By being aware of these heuristics and actively working to mitigate their effects, practitioners can make more informed and effective decisions for their patients.

Heuristics serve as an expedient way to process information and, for the most part, serve us well, but it's best to keep the above mentioned pitfalls in mind. We'll now shift our discussion to the essential topics of persuasion and influence.

The Power of Persuasion

Cialdini calls methods of persuasion the "weapons of influence" because if we're not careful, agents of persuasion can use finely tuned techniques to get us to do their bidding. Okay, perhaps I'm using some hyperbole, but it's not far from the truth. For example, a good car salesperson can spot a target a mile away. Once in their sights, they will employ one or more techniques to ensure you leave with a new vehicle. Politicians, TV evangelists, and folks who benefit from convincing us to purchase, visit, and give donations rely on these methods daily.

Many of the "weapons of influence" may be familiar to you, and you've likely experienced their power often throughout your life. Of course, you may strongly disagree whether you'd fall prey to some of these methods, but research clearly shows we're not well equipped to avoid the pull of influence. In this section, I'll begin by discussing one of the most common influential techniques, the power of reciprocity, and guide us through several others.

The Power of Reciprocity

"The more you give, the more you get." - Wayne Dyer

Have you ever received an unexpected gift from someone? Now think about your initial feelings about that exchange. Perhaps, after you said, "thank you," you said, "you didn't have to." That's a typical response. The legendary Greek philosopher Aristotle understood that "man is by nature a social animal." In this respect, when someone does something nice for us, we, in turn, feel a social obligation to do something nice for them. Cialdini says the rule of reciprocity is one of the most potent weapons of influence, stating, "the rule says that we should try to repay, in kind, what another person has provided us." If a neighbor gives us a nice bottle of wine, we feel obligated to do something nice in return; if a doctor gives us a free supplement, we feel compelled to return the favor - whether that means making sure to make the next appointment or bringing in a homemade item as a thank you. Those neglecting to conform to the rule of reciprocity face a steep social price tag, such as being seen as a moocher or freeloader and ostracized.

You've undoubtedly seen grocery store vendors giving free samples of a new snack product, maybe a new type of healthy chip. Good chances you were greeted by a smiling person offering you a taste. You succumbed to the offer, tasted the chip, had a word or two with the vendor, and felt a strong urge to purchase the bag of chips. Maybe you did, perhaps you didn't (usually the "didn't folks" said something like, "uh, I'll think about it and probably grab a bag later" - they don't). As a wholesale manager for a winery, I'd schedule off-site wine tastings where either me or one of my "wine ambassadors" would visit grocery stores or wine shops and set up an attractive table, and offer tastings. We'd set up our tasting table adorned with a lovely table cape, several bottles of wine, marketing materials, 2-for-1 tasting cards to encourage a winery visit, and my big old smiling face. The process was fascinating. Curious folks would cautiously approach my table, looking quietly at the bottles of wine, and I'd ask them if they'd like to try some of our delicious wine. The majority of tasters did try the wine, and, of course, I had an ample supply of wine I brought along so they could immediately snag a bottle or two before leaving to finish their shopping. It was highly successful.

Here are a couple of ways you could use the rule of reciprocity in your practice or business:

<u>Building An Email List</u> - applying the rule of reciprocity, a natural healthcare business could create an accessible document, such as "10 Brain Boosting Tips," a downloadable pdf that visitors to your website can download after giving their email address. See the Email Marketing section to learn more about building a successful email marketing program and automating responses.

<u>An attitude of gratitude</u> - this will come naturally to many practitioners; imagine you're a naturopathic doctor who spends extra time with a patient to fully understand their health concerns and create a personalized treatment plan. The patient may feel grateful for the amount of time and effort put in by you and may reciprocate by strictly adhering to the treatment plan (frequently a challenge), recommending you and your practice to their friends and family, or even bringing small gifts or tokens of appreciation to their next visit. In this scenario, the gratitude and giving may continue when you, the healthcare professional, reciprocate by offering additional resources or support to the client beyond what is expected.

Overall, the rule of reciprocity can create a positive cycle of mutual benefit in healthcare relationships, where both the healthcare professional and the client feel valued and supported.

Likeability

"The more we like someone, the more we are willing to do for them, and the more likely we are to be influenced by their ideas and opinions."

- Robert B. Cialdini

We were at a house party recently hosted by an organization bent on passing medical-related legislation. Like many organized parties, it began with a meet-and-greet. At this informal time, folks mingled, chatted, munchies were brought out, and people gathered in small groups. Finally, everyone was brought together into a large room for a legislative update. The information presented was interesting, the presenter charismatic, and at the end of the talk came "the ask." The requestor sought volunteers to help with the cause, and a clipboard was sent around the room for guests to leave their contact information. The cost to comply was low, simply a name and email address. As the sign-up sheet quickly filled with names, I reflected on the organizers' success at this early stage. This classic tool of persuasion has a very long and fruitful history.

Whether seeking to fill a sign-up sheet with names, collect email addresses for a new clinic, or sell Tupperware or wine at an in-home party, the fundamentals are the same.

It's not shocking to realize that we're more apt to say "yes" to those we like. But what are some of the factors that make someone "like" us?

<u>Pretty People:</u> We are hardwired to see attractive people as more talented, kind, honest, and intelligent than lesser attractive folks. This automaticity, as Caldini describes, is what social scientists call the Halo Effect. Halo Effect is an excellent example of another form of mental shortcut. In this case, the shortcut is "good looking = good." Even though we may believe attractiveness doesn't impact our decision-making process, research suggests otherwise. Canadian researchers studied this phenomenon for a national election process finding attractive candidates received two and a half times more votes than their less attractive challengers. Contrary to the evidence, the voters rejected that the candidate's attractiveness impacted their vote; instead, they were highly confident they didn't conform to this type of mental shortcut.

<u>Just Like Me</u> - Attractiveness isn't the only factor influencing our likeability. We also like people who are similar to us. We like people who are like us in terms of background, political affiliation, appearance, what we wear, and personal interests, to name a few. You may have

heard about "mirroring" - this is a technique to gain compliance with another simply by mirroring their movements, posture, intonations, and speaking style.

<u>You are Smart and Good Looking</u> - Cialdini describes the strategy of the world's "greatest car salesman," finding the secret to the salesperson's success was rooted in getting his prospects to "like him." This salesperson did what many of us never would, as it was time-consuming and costly. Each month he'd mail a postcard to everyone on his list, all 13,000 of them, to celebrate whatever holiday (e.g., Thanksgiving, Easter, New Year, President's Day) was occurring that particular month. What did the card say? Besides the monthly theme, they'd include this phrase: "I like you." Citing the research of Byrne, Rasche, & Kelly (1974), Caldini shares, "we tend, as a rule, to believe praise and like those who provide it, often when it is probably untrue."

<u>Frequency Enhances Liking</u> - Familiarity breeds liking. The more we are exposed to something, whether a person's name or a person, the more likely we will have a favorable opinion. Political strategists know this, just witness the number of times you see a candidate's name and face. The results are evident - the more we see them, the more likely they will win.

Authority

"Authority figures can be highly influential in shaping our attitudes and behaviors, and can even override our own moral judgments in certain situations." - Stanley Milgram

Authority figures possess compliance power well above those perceived with less authority. For example, we will be more likely to follow the medical advice of a naturopathic physician over the opinions of someone without medical training. Perhaps you're familiar with the compliance studies by the famed psychologist Stanley Milgram. In his infamous research program, he sought to study the effects of punishment on memory and learning; however, this was not the purpose of the study. Instead, the study sought to understand the role authority played in compliance.

In this classic study, one of the study participants was the Teacher, and the other participant was the Learner. The "Teacher" was to connect the "Learner" with electrodes to a "Shock Generator." First, the Learner had to memorize a paired series of numbers. Then, when unable to recall at a prompt, the Teacher was to push a button that administered a shock from a low-level shock, building upwards, at 15-volt increments, until 300 volts (reading: Dangerous). The Teacher and the Learner were in separate rooms connected by an intercom allowing both to communicate. In addition to the Teacher, an Authority Figure guided the process and encouraged the "Teacher" to administer shocks to incorrect answers.

Let's pull back the curtain and reveal how the researchers conducted their study. The "Learner" was a stooge, someone part of the study to test whether the "Teacher," the actual test subject of the experiment, would administer the shocks. The true purpose wasn't to learn about the effects of punishment on learning; instead, it was to explore whether a test subject would continue to administer increasingly painful shocks to another human being simply by being prompted by the "authority figure" to do so. The results were...shocking! The stooge would correctly answer a few of the prompts but then begin incorrectly answering, requiring the Teacher to shock them. The stooge would say such things as "ouch, this hurts" or "my heart hurts, please stop," only to be shocked again. This continued to happen until the stooge no longer responded to the questions and went silent - many "Teachers" continued to the end well after the "Learner" (stooge) went silent. All of this only required the "authority figure" to say things like this: "the study requires it" or "you must continue." This study illustrates the importance of institutional review boards (IRB) and ethically applying methods of influence in your business dealings.

Recognizing the power of authority, for good or naught, makes me wonder about the trappings of an authority figure and whether a business can use it for good.

<u>"I'm a Doctor" - the Power of Title</u> - Professional titles convey an immediate sense of power and authority to almost any audience. It's another mental shortcut eliciting a quick understanding that this person knows something worthwhile. Earning professional degrees requires much time, energy, and financial commitment. By the time one earns a title, such as ND, JD, DC, L.Ac, MD, Ph.D., etc., they've undergone a tremendous amount of study. Not only does a title convey a sense of power and authority, but studies have also shown that it makes people view them more significantly. Cialdini describes a study that explored the notion that title increased the perception of height. Researchers in Australia investigated the height perception of students by having a study participant pose, using a variety of academic titles, to several different classes. This person was introduced as a student in one class and other courses, as a professor, senior lecturer, and other similar titles. The findings from this study show that students viewed the "professor" versus the "student" to be two and a half inches taller. Essentially, as the title increased, they grew by ½ inch.

<u>What You Wear Matters</u> - Compliance can be increased by what you wear. For example, when an authority figure wears the outfit of the profession, they are seen as having more authority. In one study, an authority figure asked the public to comply with various requests, such as picking up trash on the street or standing on one side of a sign, from a young man dressed in street clothes or from one dressed in a security guard outfit. Regardless of the request, people were likelier to comply with someone dressed in professional garb. Using this knowledge, a

natural healthcare provider wishing to increase their perceived power could wear conventional scrubs or lab coats.

<u>Status Symbols</u>: Aside from the professional garments worn, someone can enhance authority by wearing expensive clothing, driving fancy cars, and owning large homes. Studies have shown that people are more patient with drivers of expensive cars versus those older or economy cars when waiting at a stop light after the light turns green.

Commitment & Consistency

"The commitments that bind us to our own behavior are often so powerful that they lead us to continue to behave in ways we would otherwise prefer to abandon." - Philip Zimbardo

Once we practice a behavior, we tend to stick with it because individuals tend to be viewed as flaky, unreliable, and perhaps even psychologically troubled when we deviate from a previous and consistent stance. However, researcher Cialdini writes, "once we make a choice or take a stand, we will encounter personal and interpersonal pressures to behave consistently with that commitment." He cites a research example that many of us have practiced. In this scenario, the researcher places a beach blanket and portable radio within 5 feet of another beachgoer (the experimental subject) and tests consistency and commitment by having a "thief" enter the scene.

In the first condition, shortly after setting up their beach blanket, the accomplice (the stooge helping the researcher) gets up and takes a stroll down the beach; then, a researcher posing as a "thief" approaches the blanket, takes the radio, and leaves. Not unexpectedly, in this uncommitted condition, the nearby sunbather rarely intervenes, and only 20% sought to retrieve the radio. In the other situation, the same setup is in place with one exception; the accomplice asked the neighbor to please "watch my things." In this new, committed scenario, the neighbor intervened 95% of the time.

That's great, right? Kind of. Once we've publicly committed to a position, taken a stance, or given an opinion, we go to great lengths to avoid being seen as inconsistent. The problem with this sort of thinking is that once someone decides on an issue, they tend to file it away, so when challenged by an opposing point of view - despite the quality of the argument, they revert to the automatic response and remain consistent with an earlier, and perhaps outdated position. We see this in politics, religion, business dealings, environmental issues, and healthcare. For example, suppose you are a natural healthcare provider. In that case, there's a good chance you've heard conventional medical practitioners say of alternative therapies that "there's no research to support this claim," when, in fact, there may be hundreds of research articles supporting their claim. Once someone makes up their mind, getting them to unbelieve their beliefs is challenging.

So, how can we break the consistency automaticity pattern? Cialdini discusses how social psychologists broke the code, and it's through commitment. He says someone can undo stubborn earlier consistency and commitments by getting the person to "go on the record" publicly with an updated stance. By getting someone to break with an earlier pattern, by committing publicly, there is "a natural tendency to behave in ways that are stubbornly consistent with the stand," thereby creating a new routine.

Scarcity

"The fear of missing out (FOMO) is a powerful motivator that can be leveraged to increase sales and engagement." - Nir Eyal

The McRib sandwich, for whatever reason, is a desirable food product from McDonald's and whose diehard fans eagerly await the occasional and limited-time-only release. Personally, the McRib sandwich doesn't push any of my Pavlovian buttons. Still, I understand the underlying psychological principles at work and why a company would apply this persuasion tactic. Cialdini shares his experience with the scarcity principle and suggests, "opportunities seem more valuable to us when they are less available." Intuitively that makes sense. If you want a limited amount of something, you will ensure you're first in line to get it. To illustrate the point with an example, imagine you want to see a concert, maybe you're a fan of the Dave Matthews Band, and they will be playing at a small venue in your city with limited tickets available. By understanding the power of the scarcity principle, the promoters will use familiar phrases, such as "nearly sold out" or "limited tickets available," to boost ticket sales early.

The scarcity principle works best with losing rather than gaining something. Take, for example, the research conducted by Wilson, Kaplan & Schneiderman, 1987; and Wilson, Purdon, & Wallston, 1988, when examining which perspective was most effective in getting smokers to quit. Physicians' letters to smokers describing the years they would gain if they stopped smoking were less effective than messages relating to the number of years lost if they continue smoking.

Essentially there are two varieties of the scarcity principle agents of persuasion use:

<u>Scarcity of Product</u> - We'd used this principle frequently when I worked in the wine industry. Inventory tends to accumulate when you've been producing wine for a long time. On several occasions, we'd want to clear out inventory when a particular wine was beginning to diminish, or even more practically, we'd want to boost sales during a traditionally slow period - in the wine world, that's slow sales season - that tended to begin in late January and extended into March. During this sluggish sales period, we'd promote the sales of certain wines by exclaiming such

things as "This is the last chance to get the 2013 Cabernet Sauvignon before it's gone," following up with other promotions stating, "Only 10 cases remaining, reserve your case today." The scarcity strategy works well and is used regularly in retail.

<u>Scarcity of Time</u> - Businesses also utilize the fear of missing out because of a limited window of opportunity when applying the scarcity principle. For example, a company might consider using this approach to drive traffic to a brick-and-mortar location, medical practice, or online store. This approach is used frequently to create a sense of urgency and is highly effective. A business wanting to sell a service or product wishing to develop a sense of urgency may use phrases such as "limited time offer," "sale ends Friday," or "exclusive offer to our patients, offer expires on May 5th." Interestingly enough, while writing this section, I paused to check my email and social media account and noticed this advertisement for a chiropractic franchise about to open another nearby location; it read: "A NEW location is COMING SOON near you! Claim the offer below for a FREE visit when we open. Don't delay, spots are filling up!"

Social Proof

"When in Rome, do as the Romans do." - Anonymous

When unsure how to act in a social setting, we rely on those around us to provide social cues on appropriate behavior. Examples are all around us in everyday life, such as if you're in a new city, what's the proper way to cross a street, in some places, it's common to cross the road wherever you'd like, other locales people wait at crosswalks for the illuminated sign to change. We look to other people to help guide our behaviors. If everyone at a dinner party is picking away at their barbeque chicken with a knife and fork, there is a good chance you won't pick up a leg with your hand and instead follow suit. If you're traveling along a freeway with a 60mph speed limit and everyone around is zipping along at 75mph, you'll probably adjust your speed accordingly. Other people provide easy access to acceptable behavior, and we model our behavior based on others. It's another mental shortcut we apply routinely.

According to Cialdini, the principle of social proof states, "we determine what is correct by finding out what other people think is correct." By trying to figure out the right way to act, "we view a behavior as correct in a given situation to the degree that we see others performing it."

For a time, I was an adjunct professor at a small college in Iowa, teaching Introduction to Psychology and Social Psychology and helping students learn the basics of those subjects. I'd include lectures, in-class projects and activities, written assignments, and a research project in each course. One of the classic social proof experiments was my students' favorite and followed a straightforward approach. The students worked together in pairs. For example, one student researcher was to pose outside between classes looking up towards the sky, sometimes pointing upwards.

In contrast, the other student researcher kept tabs on the behavior of passersby. They could add others to the condition by having them join the group with everyone looking up and pointing. Soon passersby would stop, join the group, chat, and look upward, trying to see what the others were looking at with excitement.

Agents of persuasion love to apply Social Proof when they use phrases such as "Best Naturopathic Doctor in Seattle" or "Best Selling Herbal Preparation" since they don't need to prove it with statistics or facts; instead, all the advertiser needs to state is that "so many others say it is," therefore, it must be true. If you've been to a coffee shop or bar, you'll often notice a tip jar stocked with a few fresh dollars. Successful baristas or bartenders know that once you prime the tip jar with a few sample bucks, customers, relying on the power of Social Proof, follow the script and behave appropriately by offering a tip.

Understanding how people process information is often seen as the key to comprehending how people can be influenced to do something, such as follow a medical order, recommendation, or treatment plan. Next, we move on to our first theoretical model often used in health behavior research, the Elaboration Likelihood Model (ELM) of Persuasion.

Elaboration Likelihood Model (ELM) of Persuasion

"The Elaboration Likelihood Model helps medical practitioners understand the factors that influence patients' attitudes and beliefs about health, and provides a basis for developing effective interventions to promote behavior change." - Robert B. Cialdini

People often behave in confusing ways and social scientists delve into the underlying reasons trying to explain why we do what we do. The Elaboration Likelihood Model (ELM) of persuasion is a helpful way to think about how people process information and make a decision. So, for example, if you're trying to create persuasive messages to change attitudes, a key to many behavioral frameworks, it's in your best interest to understand how people process information and what makes for an enduring and persuasive message.

Richard Petty and John Cacioppo, in the 1980s, created a dual-process model that explains how attitudes can be modified through persuasive communications. For example, in health communications, the messaging must be concise and compelling if hope exists for an attitude change. The Elaboration Likelihood Model of persuasion is based on the notion that people process information in one of two ways: the Central and Peripheral routes. The idea is that people process persuasive messages differently depending on how motivated or engaged they are with the message.

Figure 1. Elaboration Likelihood Model

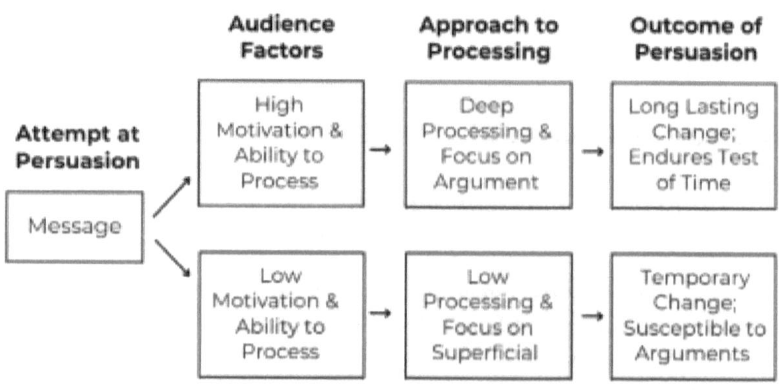

The Central Processing route happens when someone is motivated enough to critically evaluate the content of the message and delve into the science or rationale behind the claims. In this process of "elaborating" upon the persuasive message, the information becomes "sticky," resulting in deeper processing and more likely to shift an attitude. For example, a naturopathic doctor explains to a heart patient the cost/benefit of a particular course of action for a specific heart condition. The doctor describes the condition, experience, and success, then presents scientific evidence to support the claim and recommendation. Patients given these explanations tend to form more positive attitudes toward the advice and are more likely to comply.

The Peripheral Route to persuasion occurs when people use mental shortcuts and cues to determine the messenger's credibility. Cues related to attractiveness, power, or authority come into play when an individual needs to be motivated to process the information deeply. This isn't to say the peripheral route to persuasion doesn't work; it does. For people unable or unwilling to use a deeper level of cognition, the peripheral route is a shortcut to processing information. For example, a trusted and knowledgeable doctor's recommendation alone may be sufficient for a patient using the peripheral route to change their attitude, even though they may not fully understand the complexity of the science behind it.

The strength or longevity of the attitude change depends upon which processing route is followed. Central route processing messages tend to be long-lasting and resistant to counterattacks, that is, challenges to the facts surrounding the persuasive message than with the peripheral route.

Let's explore what a healthcare practitioner may experience:

Imagine a naturopathic doctor (ND) specializing in treating patients with Chronic Fatigue Syndrome (CFS). The ND has developed a new treatment protocol that includes dietary changes, herbal supplements, and lifestyle modifications that have been shown to improve CFS symptoms in previous patients.

In this example, the ND may use both routes to persuade potential patients to try their new treatment protocol. So let's consider each route in turn:

Using the Central route, the doctor may present potential patients with detailed information about the treatment protocol, including the scientific evidence behind each component of the protocol, the potential benefits and risks, and the expected outcomes. The ND may also take the time to answer any patient questions and address any concerns they may raise. By presenting this information clearly and logically, the ND appeals to the central persuasion route, which requires the patient to evaluate the information given to them carefully.

Using the Peripheral route, the ND may also use peripheral cues to persuade potential patients to try the new treatment protocol. For example, the ND may emphasize their qualifications and experience in treating CFS, highlighting their status as a licensed naturopathic doctor and their years of experience treating patients with CFS. The ND may also use testimonials from previous patients who have successfully used the protocol to improve their symptoms. By emphasizing these peripheral cues, the ND is appealing to the peripheral route of persuasion, which relies on cues that are not directly related to the content of the message.

In reality the ND will likely use a combination of both Peripheral and Central Processing routes to ensure their treatment recommendations are followed.

The ELM is an effective persuasive framework often used in health communications to persuade community members to conform to public health messages. Understanding the complexities of creating behavioral change requires a more sophisticated approach and in the following chapter we explore several of the more established models.

CHANGING MINDS, CHANGING BEHAVIORS:
Effective Strategies for Behavioral Change

We've just spent several pages exploring communication and the power of persuasion. In this coming chapter, we expand our view by exploring behavioral change models. Models of persuasion and behavioral change share a common goal of influencing human behavior, and the differences reside in the underlying assumptions and goals each theory offers. While the coming information can be a tad heady, it's one the most exciting and significant sections having the potential to make your business rise above others if thoughtfully applied. What are the differences between the theoretical model of persuasion I just covered and the behavioral change models to come?

Models of persuasion are built on the foundation that behavioral change results from the ability to influence the attitudes and beliefs of someone. The assumption is that if we, the agents of persuasion, can change the attitudes and beliefs of our audience, behavioral change will come about. Similarly, behavioral change models suggest that behavior comes from the interaction of several environmental, social, and personal factors. The goal of behavioral models of change is to understand the relationship between the elements and develop strategies that modify the aspects to create desirable behavioral change.

While quite similar, the chief differences focus on environmental and personal factors; persuasion models lean into tactics to influence attitudes and beliefs, while behavioral models focus on specific interventions to influence behavior.

Social Psychology to the Rescue

Understanding how people think, feel, and behave is crucial to living in everyday social situations. If you're a healthcare professional having insights into why people do what they do, for example, why some patients follow your recommendations and others do not, can tremendously impact the efficacy of your practice and the health of your patients or clients. Imagine if you could anticipate potential roadblocks to compliance, build communities to improve health outcomes, and create effective communications that drive traffic and influence the behaviors (in the most positive and ethical of ways) of your patients and clients.

As a doctoral student, I studied the intricacies of "wilderness experience" for four long and fun years. Consequently, I became familiar with the most compelling theoretical frameworks in cognitive psychology, social psychology, and communication theory. This arduous academic journey commenced with delving into the research literature, discussing the current state of knowledge, determining how my study could integrate those ideas, and going out into the field to study backcountry visitors using in-depth interviews, in-situ surveys, as well as observe visitor behavior, and generally spend a whole lot of time in some extraordinarily gorgeous wilderness locations in the states of Washington and Oregon. The view from my office, a tent in the wilderness, wasn't too shabby!

Since those days, I've had the chance to apply the academic knowledge I learned and used in the field to my roles in several industries: as a college instructor of psychology, in the wineries where I worked as a marketer and wholesale manager, and in my consulting businesses with great success.

Social psychology investigates how human beings think, feel, and behave in everyday social situations. Therefore, understanding the principles of social psychology, and having a basic comprehension of the coming theoretical models, can be incredibly beneficial to any natural healthcare business. Here are a few reasons why:

<u>Improved Compliance</u>: Social psychologists have learned that people are more likely to follow your course of treatment (medical recommendations) when the healthcare professional's messages are consistent with the beliefs and values of the patients. Therefore, using tailored health messages to different target audiences will increase the chances of positive behavioral change.

<u>Improved Effectiveness with Group Support</u>: Research suggests behavioral change is more effective when the interventions include social support and group participation. By having these interventions, your practice is more likely to increase the effectiveness of treatment plans.

<u>Engaging in Healthy Behaviors</u>: It is clear that when we aim to get our patients or clients to engage in positive health behaviors, they will be more likely to be successful when they are part of a community that supports and values those behaviors. When a practice creates a supportive and inclusive space and builds a supportive community, healthier behaviors will likely result.

Next, we'll shift our attention to our most fundamental beliefs about ourselves and our ability to accomplish tasks.

Self-Efficacy & Locus of Control

As I will explain, an individual's ability to complete a task or adhere to a treatment plan may be impacted by their beliefs regarding their ability to attain it and manage the process.

The belief in one's ability to complete a task or reach a goal is known as self-efficacy. For example, suppose someone doesn't believe they can follow through with a healthcare plan a provider recommends. In that case, it is likely they will not accomplish the goal. People with high self-efficacy tend to have increased motivation, are more persistent in working towards goals, and are resilient when faced with difficulties and obstacles while working towards their goals. Conversely, someone with low self-efficacy can be plagued by feelings associated with anxiety, helplessness, and avoidance.

Similarly, locus of control refers to someone's belief that they have control over the situations in their life. Folks with an internal locus of control believe they have control over it. In contrast, those with an external locus of control feel outside forces are responsible for what happens to them. These powerful concepts will frequently appear in the psychological models that will soon follow.

By understanding these important concepts, practitioners can better understand the roadblocks to compliance and utilize methods to increase the likelihood that a patient or client will be successful. Furthermore, the research is clear, those with an internal locus of control are more likely to follow the advice of a practitioner. For example, a study published in the Journal of Health Psychology in 2010 found that people with an internal locus of control were more likely to follow through with the treatment protocols for chronic diseases such as diabetes and hypertension than those with an external locus of control.

Cognitive Dissonance

Have you ever wondered why some people continue to smoke cigarettes when it's clear they understand the health consequences and, despite that, continue to smoke anyway? People are confusingly interesting to me, and it's likely you're at least somewhat familiar with the concept of cognitive dissonance. In music, dissonance means "lack of harmony among musical notes," and in social psychology, cognitive dissonance is a theory used to explain why people behave in inconsistent ways.

In the 1950's social psychologist Leon Festinger offered a theoretical framework suggesting people feel a sense of discomfort when they possess conflicting beliefs or attitudes (e.g., smoking is bad, and yet, I still smoke) and seek to find ways to alleviate their discomfort by adopting either an attitude or behavior change.

Let's explore an example of someone who wants to be healthier by eating a healthy, balanced diet; however, they still enjoy candy bars, soda, and fatty snacks. The cognitive dissonance caused by holding these conflicting thoughts and behaviors can lead them to experience this tension. The individual may experience feelings of guilt when consuming junk food even though they wish to be more healthy; alternatively, they may shift thoughts and begin to rationalize their behaviors by saying to themselves, "it's okay if I only have this once in a while." Consequently, the person may change their attitude about junk food, such as "an occasional soda is okay," or they may change their behavior and no longer eat junk food.

People go to dramatic lengths to appear to be consistent with their attitudes and behavior because when we appear inconsistent, others may view the person as flaky or potentially troubled. To minimize this discomfort or inconsistency when holding contradictory attitudes, beliefs, or ideas, people will use a variety of cognitive dissonance strategies, such as:

<u>Denial</u>: Patients or clients may deny or not acknowledge information conflicting with their attitudes or beliefs. Imagine a patient who wants to live a healthy lifestyle but refuses to accept the facts surrounding alcohol usage or eating manufactured food. What can you do? In the Elaboration Likelihood Model (ELM) of persuasion, in the previous chapter, I described how people process information - central and

peripheral routes. The central route of processing information tends to produce longer-term behavioral change. With this knowledge, it'd be essential to work with your patient by providing scientific evidence to support them and guide them with evidence and real-world examples.

<u>Selective exposure</u>: This is a classic way to deal with the inconsistency between our thoughts and actions. Using the selective exposure strategy, one chooses to expose themselves to messages and information consistent with their behaviors. We see this often in partisan news outlets with viewers and listeners choosing stations that support their political views. For those wanting to live a healthy lifestyle, it may mean they avoid news stories about unhealthy lifestyle choices. Alternatively, they may stop hanging out with friends or families that continue to follow unhealthy lifestyle choices.

<u>Rationalization</u>: Many people deal with their feelings of cognitive dissonance discomfort by using a strategy that attempts to explain away or justify the consistency between their attitudes and behaviors. Rationalization is a common practice among those who seek a way to justify their dissonant behaviors. Take, for example, a patient named John, who's been trying to lose weight, get healthy, and be able to hike a local trail that he's been unable to for the past several years. In this instance, John tends to overly rely on rationalization to avoid taking control of his health by saying to his healthcare provider, "I only eat the Snickers bar when I need the energy, you know, late at night or early in the morning to get my day going." At this point, the healthcare provider should remind John of his goals, that the rationalization strategy is holding him back, and that eating junk food at those particular times is working against his health plan.

<u>Confirmation bias</u>: This concept may seem familiar because I mentioned the idea in the heuristics section in the earlier chapter on communication and persuasion. Like the strategy of selective exposure,

those who rely on confirmation bias tend to seek information that "confirms" their existing beliefs and ignore anything that contradicts them. We tend to be attracted to information, people, news, and groups that agree with us and avoid things that cause us to question our beliefs or challenge our perceptions. It's a handy mental shortcut but one that can cause our patients or clients problems. Imagine a patient wishing to improve their cognitive function and is "cherry picking" the information they read or watch. Only choosing stories that reinforce their current opinions without regard to differing opinions is practicing confirmation bias and is harmful to patient health.

Compartmentalization: This strategy separates one's attitudes and beliefs into different compartments, allowing people to live without dealing with their behavioral inconsistencies. Patients and clients may compartmentalize their health-supportive behaviors (i.e., eating well, exercising, drinking adequate water) and unhealthy behaviors (i.e., smoking, alcohol drinking, and cannabis consumption).

To encourage your patients and clients to live a healthy lifestyle, it's essential to help them understand the concept of cognitive dissonance and the strategies we use to justify unhealthy behaviors. Encourage your patients to seek contradictory information that challenges their preexisting beliefs, try to be open to alternative points of view, and be willing to keep an open mind. Inspire them to build a supportive community that shares common values and goals and create a pattern of behaviors that support a positive mindset seeing challenges as temporary setbacks all designed to help them grow and learn rather than as a failure.

Undoubtedly, human behavior is an intricate tapestry, and the preceding sections and chapters of this book have skillfully laid the groundwork upon which we will build a more profound comprehension of the intricacies behind people's actions. As healthcare professionals, aiding our patients and clients in reaching their health objectives necessitates delving into the depths of behavioral psychology. It demands our unwavering dedication and concerted effort as we navigate the vast expanse of our current knowledge. By immersing ourselves in this process, we will gain invaluable insights that will enable us to better comprehend how and why individuals behave the way they do, ultimately empowering us to facilitate meaningful behavior change.

Much of the research on behavior change focuses on "why" behavior change occurs; however, before we delve into those models, I want to pause to elaborate on a model that addresses "how" behavior change occurs. The Transtheoretical Model of Change (TMC) describes how people change behavior.

Transtheoretical Model of Change

"The stages of change provide a roadmap for individuals and practitioners to navigate the complex journey of behavior change, acknowledging that change happens in incremental steps." - Carlo C. DiClemente

The Transtheoretical Model of Change (TMC), also known as the The Stages of Behavioral Change, is a theory created by psychologists James O. Prochaska and Carlo C. DiClemente. It helps us understand how people go through different stages when they want to change their behavior. Many fields, like health psychology, addiction counseling, and behavior change interventions, use this model.

According to this model, behavior change doesn't happen suddenly. Instead, it occurs in a series of distinct stages. It's important to note that these stages are not always followed in a straight line, and individuals may go back and forth between them. Let's look at each stage more closely:

<u>Precontemplation</u>: In this stage, individuals are not aware that they need to change or they don't believe change is necessary. They may ignore or resist suggestions or information about their behavior. For example, a smoker who has no intention of quitting would be in the precontemplation stage.

<u>Contemplation</u>: In this stage, individuals realize they have a problem and start considering the possibility of change. They weigh the advantages and disadvantages of changing their behavior. For instance, someone who's thinking about quitting smoking might think about the health benefits and the challenges they might face.

<u>Preparation</u>: In the preparation stage, individuals commit to making a change and are ready to take action. They may start taking small steps towards modifying their behavior or gather information and resources to support their change efforts. For example, someone planning to quit smoking might research cessation methods or set a quit date.

<u>Action</u>: This stage involves actively modifying one's behavior to achieve the desired change. People in the action stage make visible changes and implement strategies to maintain their new behavior. For instance, someone trying to lose weight might follow a specific diet and exercise plan.

<u>Maintenance</u>: The maintenance stage occurs when individuals have successfully changed their behavior and work to prevent relapse. This stage requires ongoing effort and commitment to sustain the new behavior over time. For example, someone who has quit smoking and actively avoids triggers would be in the maintenance stage.

<u>Termination</u>: Not all versions of the model include this stage, but in some cases, termination represents the point where the new behavior becomes ingrained, and there is no temptation or risk of returning to

the old behavior. At this stage, the change has become a permanent part of the individual's lifestyle.

It's important to recognize that relapse is common during behavior change, and individuals may regress to previous stages. However, relapse is seen as an opportunity for learning, not a failure. The model acknowledges that change is a process that requires time, effort, and support.

The Stages of Behavioral Change model helps us understand individuals' readiness to change and allows practitioners to design interventions based on their stage. By recognizing the stage a person is in, natural healthcare professionals can develop strategies to facilitate progress and increase the chances of successful behavior change.

We've covered several important aspects of social psychology used to describe the roots of behavior and justifications we use to explain away our behavioral actions. Now we're going to shift our emphasis to the "why's" of behavior change by trying to explain the underlying constructs of persuasion and behavioral change. As a business owner, it's essential to understand how people process information, make decisions, and persuade a client or customer to do the right thing. Doing the right thing could be as straightforward as getting a monthly massage or annual physical or as complex as changing your smoking behavior. We'll begin this exploration by reviewing a foundational model, the Expectancy Value (EV) model, that many are based upon.

Expectancy Value (EV) Models

Have you ever wondered why your patients or clients don't follow through with your medical orders or recommendations? It's easy to fall prey to the belief that some of your patients or clients don't care by using mental shortcuts yourself. Of course, the reasons why people behave as they do have captured the attention of psychologists for a very long time and continue to challenge the best of us.

Understanding how and why people behave as they do has intrigued human beings for eons, attempting to build basic models to make sense of human behavior. One of the earliest theoretical frameworks to explain the decision-making process comes from a family of theories called the Expectancy-Value (EV) theories. In their book "Health Behavior Theory for Public Health," authors DiClemente, Salazar, and Crosby (2013) discuss how EV theories, an umbrella term for several models, explain how people weigh pluses and minuses for any given decision in an attempt to maximize benefits. The authors state, "people will change a behavior if they anticipate the personal benefits derived from the outcome will outweigh any 'costs' incurred through enacting the behavior," and suggest people use "mental math" to quickly calculate a cost-benefit analysis before making a decision.

The desirability of a cost-benefit model for decision-making tends to lose its attractiveness once costs and benefits become clearer. Both costs and benefits can also include social, emotional, and physical factors, making the model more complex. For example, DiClemente and colleagues state, "all too often, health promotion programs focus only on the physical benefits of a given health behavior." Consider it momentarily: how often have you solely relied on a physical benefit, such as losing weight, to minimize the risk of cardiovascular problems? While vital and indeed a worthwhile goal, when folks try to lose weight, it's also for other related reasons, such as social reasons or wanting to lose weight for appearance. In addition to the complexity of costs and benefits are our perceptions of the immediacy of the costs and benefits. The previous example still holds. The perception of "prospective gains and averted loss" will play a role. For example, the social benefits people have from losing weight are more apt to appear more quickly, increasing the perception that they are better looking, an added gain. In contrast, the benefit of reducing the chance of a heart attack represents a form of avoided loss. Therefore, "perceptions about benefits may take the form of prospective gains or averted losses."

I realize some of this information is rather dense, and I hope you hang with me as I try to make it as understandable as possible. You're not alone if the content in the communication and behavior chapters makes your brain hurt a little (or a lot). I've been there myself and recall the first day of graduate school when several new graduate students and I gathered in a small conference room after reading our first set of research articles. As a seminar class, we were to read the material and return with our interpretations and understandings, taking turns sharing our perspectives. I recall one of my colleagues stated, "I didn't understand anything except the word "there." Yes, the material was complex, but the theoretical frameworks became clearer after a while. I've grown to appreciate the work that went into creating them. Since those days, I have successfully applied this 'secret knowledge' to help shape the messaging, promotions, and advertisements for many businesses and organizations. So, just like me, you'll be able to do the same once you get your head around the material, hang in there; you'll get it!

During graduate school, I was introduced to several social cognitive theories used by researchers and agents of influence to predict and shape behavioral change. Since many behavioral change models are available to review, I will focus on the foundational models. Such models could be useful to your understanding to help your patients achieve their health goals. Frankly, I want to make sure my readers aren't overloaded with information. So, instead, I want to focus on frameworks that benefit your business and practice goals. Let's begin with an old favorite, the Theory of Reasoned Action.

Theory of Reasoned Action

"The Theory of Reasoned Action recognizes the importance of understanding patients' beliefs and attitudes in promoting behavior change, and provides a useful framework for medical practitioners to tailor their interventions to the specific needs and characteristics of individual patients." - Peter Gollwitzer

Theoretical models used to explain and predict human behavior are crucial for those in the healthcare field because if we can accurately predict or understand the processes people use to decide whether or not they'll follow a health protocol, we'll be more successful in removing the obstacles to compliance. The Theory of Reasoned Action offers a framework for understanding how attitudes and subjective norms shape behavior.

Psychologists Icek Ajzen and Martin Fishbein developed the Theory of Reasoned Action (TRA) model in 1975 to explain certain behaviors. They wanted to use the ideas of the Expectancy-Value (EV) model in a more advanced way. According to this model, our behavior is influenced by our intention to do a certain thing. This intention is shaped by our attitudes toward the behavior and what we think our social group will think about it. Our attitudes are based on our beliefs about the behavior and how we evaluate it. The subjective norms in the model refer to our perceptions of whether our social group will approve of the behavior. These perceptions come from the opinions of people we value, like our family, friends, professionals, or religious community. We feel motivated to follow these opinions and behave accordingly.

Figure 2. Theory of Reasoned Action

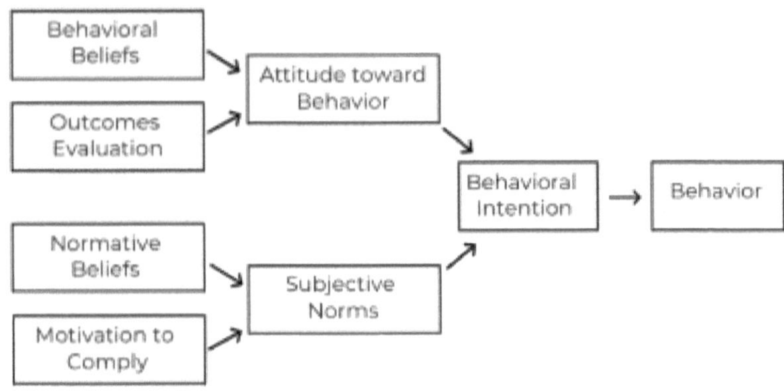

Let's work through an example to make more sense of the TRA framework. Imagine you have a 45-year-old female patient, whom we'll call Rochelle, complaining of bloating, eczema, painful gas, and general gastrointestinal problems. You've recently diagnosed them with grain intolerance. As their healthcare provider, you recommend that Rochelle modify her diet by removing grains from her diet. Rochelle reports that grain represents a significant part of her family's diet, from pasta and pancakes to bread. Her kids love peanut butter sandwiches and spaghetti. Getting our heads around the TRA requires us, the practitioner, to delve into her beliefs about the behavior (removing grain from her diet), ultimately shaping her attitude towards the behavior. Rochelle may initially form an attitude about her grain intolerance, about giving up the grain. Then she'd ponder her beliefs about going grain-free and how difficult it may be to find a suitable replacement for grain (and depending on where she lives, finding a grain substitute may be difficult). Finally, Rochelle will make a good versus bad evaluation of the behavior under consideration. She may feel adequate substitutes are available at the market, the replacements are of equal tastiness, and her kids will like it too. Researchers often use a Likert scale (say, -3 to +3) to assess health beliefs. Still, in the office, you can get a feel for this by asking relevant questions about specific health behavior beliefs and attitudes. (Hang tight, I have an example coming up that'll clarify this assessment).

As I previously mentioned, in this model, the intention to perform a behavior is predicated by attitudes (fed by one's beliefs) and subjective norms (whether we feel supported by our community). Our beliefs and attitudes may align to suggest we intend to make a behavioral change and, in this example, remove grain from Rochelle's diet. Additionally, one's subjective norms, the perceptions we have about what other people (e.g., family, friends, and colleagues) think about the social acceptability of the proposed behavioral change, is a meaningful precursor to intention.

Rochelle will weigh the normative beliefs of those she holds in high regard and then consider their opinion with her willingness to follow along with those opinions. The social pressure to conform is powerful and plays an essential role in this model. EV models rely on weighing the pros and cons of engaging in a behavioral change. The subjective norms include our perceptions of others' beliefs about the behavioral change we desire. For example, maybe Rochelle believes her friends do not want her to change. Still, the truth may be hidden because one of her best friends also struggles with adopting a gluten-free diet. Uncovering these hidden perceptions may pave the way for behavioral change. Let's continue with this example and see how Rochell may proceed.

Rochelle's attitude and subjective norms about eliminating grain from her diet was assessed. First, let's look at her attitudes toward this proposed behavioral change.

- Removing grain from my diet will likely reduce or eliminate my discomfort (rated as very positive, +3)

- Buying alternative forms of grains will be difficult (rated as highly negative, -3); she's worried she won't be able to find a suitable replacement

- Gluten free breads are hard to find where she lives (-3)

- A gluten-free diet may be socially undesirable in her community (-3)

- A diet free of grains will improve the quality of my life (+3)

Similarly, we evaluate Rochelles' subjective norms about taking on a gluten-free diet.

- My husband supports my decision to modify my diet (+3)

- My kids are supportive of this change, but may complain (+2)

- My friends tell me I ought to follow the directions of my doctor (+1)

- My doctor wants me to follow this new approach (+2)

- My dearest friend strongly supports this modification to my diet and has already bought me some gluten-free bread, and it tastes good (+3)

By assessing someone's intention to engage in a specific behavior, we'll need to consider the behavioral time frame (create a particular time frame), action required (find a grain replacement for each meal that ordinarily contains grain), desired outcome (intention to follow a grain-free diet), and context (meal or snack times).

The model could be better. In their book Social Cognition, Susan T. Fiske and Shelley E. Taylor (1991) acknowledged the value of the Theory of Reasoned Action, highlighting that "specific behavioral intentions predict specific behaviors very well" in the model; however, there is also criticism of one's "intention" to do something and the "expectation" of doing it. For example, having the knowledge that someone has the "intention" to take a hike this weekend is less meaningful than knowing a person's expectation, "I probably won't hike this weekend, since I rarely do," isn't captured in the model.

Attitudes and subjective norms are reasonably good indicators of behavioral intention; however, there are times when a patient may have supportive attitudes and subjective norms that'd suggest behavioral change is imminent but do not come to pass. Rochelle, for example, may have a solid social support system in place (subjective norms) and have positive beliefs and attitudes indicating a positive intention toward the behavioral change; however, she may also have trouble finding a suitable replacement for grains, or she may not have adequate financial resources to find proper substitutions.

Earlier in this chapter, we discussed the concepts of self-efficacy and locus of control. It's this lack of perceived control that led researchers to modify the TRA with a new construct, perceived behavioral control, and a modified model known as the Theory of Planned Behavior.

Theory of Planned Behavior (TPB)

"The Theory of Planned Behavior has been applied to a wide range of health behaviors, including smoking, physical activity, and dietary behaviors, and has been shown to be effective in promoting behavior change." - Heather Patrick

The Theory of Planned Behavior extends the Theory of Reasoned Action. It is a social cognitive theory designed to help explain human behavior by considering one's attitude, social normative factors, and perceived behavioral control. Adding a new construct, perceived behavioral control, expands our understanding of how people make decisions related to behavioral change.

As you may recall, self-efficacy focuses on one's ability to achieve a task or goal successfully. Perceived behavioral control expands that notion to include several related factors, including facilitating factors, inhibiting factors, and perceived aspects of power. Perceived behavioral control, according to DiClemente and others (2013), is the "extent to which a person or a group of people perceive that they can control the outcome, meaning that change is within their control."

Perceived behavioral control consists of several related factors: facilitating factors, inhibiting factors, and perceived power. facilitating factors represent real or perceived external factors that increase the likelihood of the specific behavior; inhibiting factors work in the other direction and are external forces that reduce the likelihood; and perceived power represents the potency of both the facilitating and inhibiting factors.

Figure 3. Theory of Planned Behavior

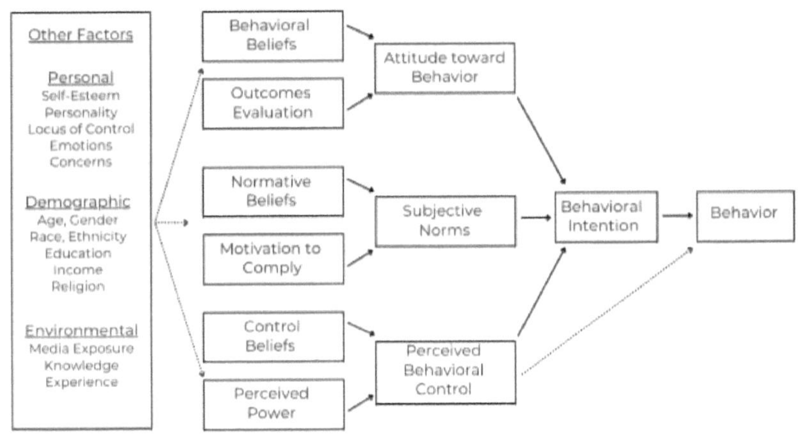

Let's take the TPB out for a test drive using Rochelle as our example. We've seen that Rochelle has positive beliefs and attitudes about her new diet. She has a supportive network of friends and family (subjective norms), indicating a positive intention toward the proposed behavioral change. Now, let's consider the concept of perceived behavioral control (PBC) to see how this new construct and factors play a role in her ultimate decision to follow through with the dietary change. We begin by weighing the facilitating and inhibiting factors:

Potential facilitating factors relative to grain replacement:

- Gluten-free grains and breads are tasty

- My family supports the change in grains

- My local grocery store has a few options

Potential inhibiting factors relative to grain replacement:

- Worry about availability of replacements when dining out

- Finding a wide selection in my community is difficult

- The price of gluten-free products is higher than traditional products

The perceived power of any single facilitating and inhibiting factor can be decisive. Take, for example, if the expense of diet modification is perceived to be too high, it doesn't matter if someone has the right attitude and positive normative factors (supportive community); the ability to pay the price for the behavioral change may outweigh everything else.

Behavioral change models are helpful in understanding how people adopt new behaviors.

The Health Belief Model (HBM)

"The Health Belief Model has been used successfully to promote behavior change in a wide range of health-related areas, including disease prevention, health promotion, and illness management." - Irwin M. Rosenstock

Figure 4. Health Belief Model

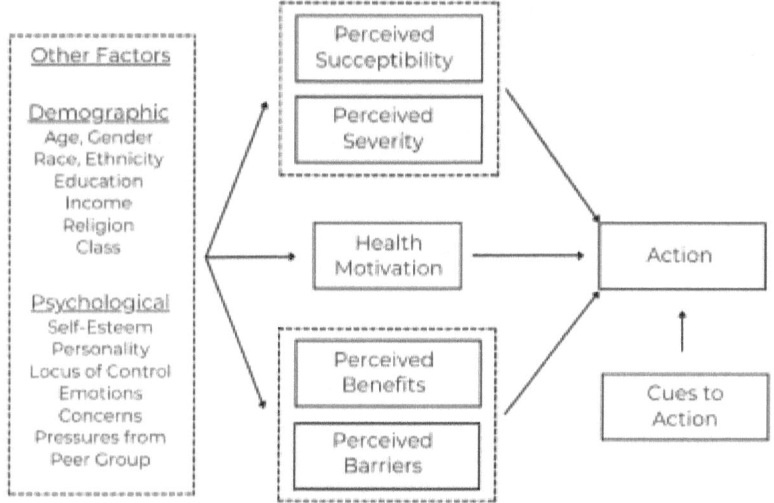

The Health Belief Model (HBM) was created by public health officials more than half a century ago to screen for the determinants of tuberculosis (DiClemente et al., 2013). As an EV model, the Health Belief Model posits that people weigh the cost and benefit of a given health decision. In other words, a mental math calculation of the expected net gain is weighed against the perceived threat level, which then determines the likelihood of behavioral change.

If you are a natural healthcare provider you can apply the Health Belief Model in practice by considering and addressing the following key elements:

<u>Perceived susceptibility</u>: This refers to how individuals perceive their vulnerability to a health condition. A doctor can ask questions like, "Do you think you are at risk of developing this condition?" or "How likely do you feel that this health issue could affect you?" By exploring patients' beliefs about their susceptibility, doctors can understand their concerns and tailor their communication accordingly.

<u>Perceived severity</u>: This aspect relates to individuals' perception of the seriousness of a health condition. Healthcare providers can inquire, "How do you view the impact of this condition on your overall health and well-being?" or "What do you think are the potential consequences of not addressing this health issue?" Understanding patients' perceived severity helps doctors highlight the importance of taking action and engaging in preventive or treatment measures.

<u>Perceived benefits</u>: Natural healthcare providers can discuss the potential benefits of adopting recommended health behaviors or treatments. They can explain, "By making these changes or following this treatment plan, you can improve your quality of life and reduce the risk of complications." Highlighting the advantages helps patients see the value in taking action and motivates them to make positive health choices.

<u>Perceived barriers</u>: It's essential to address patients' perceived barriers to taking recommended actions. Caregivers can ask, "What do you think might prevent you from following this advice or treatment plan?" or "What challenges do you anticipate in making these changes?" By identifying barriers such as financial concerns, lack of time, or personal beliefs, doctors can work collaboratively with patients to develop strategies to overcome these obstacles.

<u>Cues to action</u>: Doctors can provide cues or prompts that remind patients to take action. This could involve suggesting specific steps, providing educational materials, or referring patients to support resources. For example, a physician might say, "I encourage you to set a reminder on your phone to take your medication every day," or "Here's a brochure with tips and resources to help you quit smoking."

<u>Self-efficacy</u>: It's important to address patients' belief in their ability to successfully engage in recommended behaviors. Providers can ask, "Do you feel confident in your ability to make these changes?" or "What

support or resources do you think would help you succeed?" By acknowledging patients' self-efficacy concerns and offering encouragement, doctors can foster a sense of empowerment and motivation.

By integrating these elements into their everyday conversations with patients, doctors can effectively apply the Health Belief Model. This approach helps personalize the communication, understand patients' perspectives, and tailor interventions to enhance patients' motivation, engagement, and overall health outcomes.

Real World Example

The pandemic serves as an excellent illustration of how public health agencies could have used the HBM to encourage citizens to get a Covid-19 vaccine. In the Health Belief Model, two factors account for much of the model's power, the first being the perceived threat, which assesses the threat in terms of severity and susceptibility. The perceived severity factor refers to the evaluation someone makes about the potential badness if the illness is contracted. For this particular virus, the range of severity ranged from low to grave, with the potential of not contracting the virus, experiencing only a few symptoms to the other extreme, severe illness and even death. The perceived threat assessment also includes the perceived susceptibility evaluation. This factor, perceived susceptibility, assesses the chances of catching the "bug" and is viewed along a continuum, from low chances to highly likely.

Overall, the perceived threat is a mental calculation of the potential severity of the illness weighed against the chances of catching the virus. This cost vs. benefit model also recognizes other important factors people consider when making a pro-health behavioral change, such as modifying factors, cues to action, and an overall evaluation of the net benefit of getting the shot.

Modifying factors, such as age, race, socio-economic status, gender, and knowledge, all mediate the threat perception. For example, one's background, knowledge, and social group all impact the likelihood of following a public health recommendation. But what happens when we do our best to ensure compliance with a health recommendation, such as getting a vaccine, and the public needs to follow along? The answer is a fear appeal. Fear messages, when appropriately applied, can significantly increase compliance for a population or a group resistant to following the guidance of a health campaign. In addition, fear statements can shift the susceptibility threat assessment by applying conditional statements to messaging campaigns, such as "If you got the shot this spring, how likely is it you'd catch Covid-19?"

For fear appeals to have their most significant impact, it's essential to ensure the fear message doesn't freeze-up the people they were targeting. To be effective, create fear messages that show a way out, not so fear-inducing that it freezes people to the point where they cannot comply.

The Cues to Action come from multiple sources, such as the television news, which warns about an impending uptick of the virus, a message or reminder from a trusted healthcare provider, about something the patient experienced.

Therefore the threat perception is mediated by modifying factors and cues to action leading to an assessment of the overall expected net benefit of getting a Covid-19 vaccine, which, when taken together, yields a behavior (likelihood of getting a vaccine). At this time, 81% of Americans received at least one dose of the Covid-19 vaccination, and 69% received at least two doses (USAFACTS).

As with all behavioral change models, there are limitations. The model:

- doesn't take into consideration a person's attitude, opinions, or beliefs

- misses habitual behaviors (e.g., smoking and drinking) which moderate decision making

- lacks economic or environmental factors that can impact health behaviors

- works under the assumption that everyone has the same access to information

- assumes that the cues to action are universally supportive of the health recommendations.

Theoretical models are intended to be parsimonious; that is, the goal of a model is to keep the framework as simple and harmonious as possible, with a minimum number of factors to help describe the phenomenon. No model is perfect, and despite potential limitations, this model performs quite well and is worth keeping both the positive and negative aspects in mind when trying to encourage patients to follow a pro-health behavior.

Health Promotion Model (HPM)

"The Health Promotion Model provides a comprehensive and holistic approach to promoting health and preventing disease, and can be applied across a range of settings, populations, and health issues." - Patricia Rieker

The Health Promotion Model (HPM) is a theoretical framework developed by nursing theorist Nola J. Pender. It was first proposed in the 1980s and has since been widely used in nursing and health promotion research. The HPM is based on the idea that health promotion is a positive, proactive approach to enhancing well-being and preventing illness. It emphasizes the importance of individual characteristics, experiences, and beliefs in shaping health-related behaviors.

The Health Promotion Model consists of several key components:

<u>Individual Characteristics and Experiences</u>: This component recognizes that each individual has unique personal characteristics, such as age, gender, genetics, and socioeconomic status, which can influence their health behaviors. It also considers the individual's past experiences, including their knowledge, perceptions, and beliefs about health.

<u>Behavior-Specific Cognitions and Affect</u>: This component focuses on the cognitive and affective factors that influence health behaviors. It includes perceived benefits (the individual's beliefs about the positive outcomes of engaging in a behavior), perceived barriers (the individual's beliefs about the obstacles or negative consequences of engaging in a behavior), and self-efficacy (the individual's confidence in their ability to perform a behavior successfully).

<u>Behavioral Outcomes</u>: This component refers to individuals' actions or behaviors to promote their health. These behaviors can be health-enhancing, such as exercising regularly, eating a balanced diet, or practicing safe sex, or they can be health-compromising, such as smoking or engaging in risky behaviors.

<u>Commitment to Plan of Action</u>: This component highlights the individual's commitment to improving health. It involves setting goals, planning, and promoting behavior change strategies.

<u>Immediate and Future Health Outcomes</u>: This component focuses on the effects of health behaviors on both immediate and long-term health outcomes. Immediate outcomes include improved physical fitness, reduced stress, and increased self-esteem. In contrast, long-term

consequences may involve reduced risk of chronic diseases, increased life expectancy, or enhanced quality of life.

<u>Influencing Factors</u>: The Health Promotion Model also recognizes that various external and internal factors can influence an individual's health behaviors. These factors can be classified into two categories:

- <u>Interpersonal Influences</u>: These include social support from family, friends, and healthcare providers, as well as cultural and social norms that shape health behaviors.

- <u>Situational Influences</u>: These encompass the physical environment, such as access to healthcare facilities, availability of resources, and community support.

The Health Promotion Model emphasizes the interaction between these components and the dynamic nature of health behaviors. It suggests that individuals are more likely to engage in health-promoting behaviors when they perceive the benefits to outweigh the barriers and have a high self-efficacy level. Additionally, social support and the presence of enabling factors in the environment can facilitate positive health outcomes.

Overall, the Health Promotion Model provides a comprehensive framework for understanding and promoting health behaviors by considering individuals' unique characteristics, experiences, and beliefs, as well as the social and environmental influences on their choices.

Figure 5. Health Promotions Model

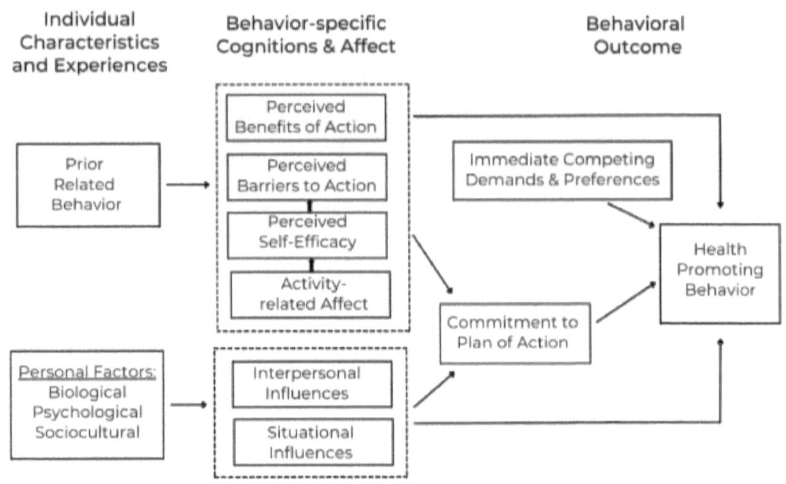

Here's how a natural healthcare provider can apply the Health Promotion Model in practice:

<u>Individual characteristics and experiences</u>: Providers can explore patients' unique characteristics and experiences that may influence their health behaviors. They can ask questions such as, "Tell me about your past experiences with trying to make changes in your health," or "What factors do you think have influenced your health behaviors in the past?" By understanding patients' individual backgrounds, healthcare providers can better tailor interventions to their specific needs and challenges.

<u>Perceived benefits of action</u>: A caregiver can discuss the potential benefits of adopting health-promoting behaviors. They can explain, "By incorporating regular exercise into your routine, you can increase your energy levels and improve your overall fitness," or "Eating a balanced diet can help you maintain a healthy weight and reduce the risk of chronic diseases." Emphasizing the positive outcomes helps patients see the value of engaging in health-promoting behaviors.

<u>Perceived barriers to action</u>: Doctors should explore patients' perceived barriers that may hinder their adoption of healthy behaviors. They can ask questions like, "What challenges do you anticipate in making these changes?" or "What obstacles might get in the way of you implementing these behaviors?" By identifying barriers such as lack of time, financial constraints, or lack of social support, physicians can collaborate with patients to develop strategies to overcome these challenges.

<u>Self-efficacy</u>: It's important for doctors to address patients' confidence in their ability to engage in health-promoting behaviors. They can ask questions like, "How confident do you feel about incorporating these changes into your daily life?" or "What support or resources do you think would help you succeed?" By acknowledging and bolstering patients' self-efficacy, doctors can empower them to take ownership of their health and feel more confident in making positive changes.

<u>Interpersonal influences</u>: Care providers should recognize the impact of interpersonal relationships on patients' health behaviors. They can inquire, "Are there any family members, friends, or colleagues who could support you in adopting these behaviors?" or "Have you discussed your health goals with anyone in your social circle?" By encouraging patients to involve supportive individuals, providers can help create an environment that fosters healthy behaviors and provides a network of encouragement.

<u>Situational influences</u>: Doctors should consider the situational factors that can either facilitate or hinder patients' health behaviors. They can discuss the influence of the physical and social environment on patients' choices and actions. For example, they might say, "How can we modify your home environment to make it easier for you to engage in healthy eating?" or "What strategies can we develop to navigate social situations that may involve unhealthy behaviors?" By addressing

situational influences, doctors can help patients proactively plan for and overcome potential obstacles.

By incorporating these elements into their conversations with patients, healthcare providers can effectively apply the Health Promotion Model. This approach allows providers to gain a holistic understanding of patients' needs, tailor interventions accordingly, and empower patients to engage in health-promoting behaviors that lead to improved overall well-being.

Now, we'll shift our focus on another theory that focuses on health threats and the motivations patients use to deal with them.

Protection Motivation Theory (PMT)

The protection motivation theory has been widely used in public health campaigns to promote behaviors that prevent or reduce the risk of various health threats, such as smoking, HIV/AIDS, and cancer." - Mark Conner

The Protection Motivation Theory (PMT) is used to understand how people respond to health threats and how they can be motivated to engage in health-promoting behaviors. According to this theory, people are motivated to protect themselves from threats that they perceive to be significant, such as health threats, by engaging in behaviors that reduce the threat. PMT suggests that people's decision to engage in health-promoting behaviors is influenced by two main factors: the Perceived Threat and the Perceived Efficacy of the recommended behavior.

The perceived threat includes two components: the severity of the threat and the likelihood of it occurring. The perceived efficacy consists of two parts: the perceived effectiveness of the recommended behavior and the perceived ease of adopting the recommended behavior. The theory suggests that when people perceive a high threat and perceive the recommended behavior as effective and easy to adopt, they are more likely to engage.

To encourage their patients to get screened for colon cancer, naturopathic doctors can use PMT to guide their communication with their patients. For example, an ND could explain to their patients that colon cancer is a severe threat and is one of the leading causes of cancer-related deaths in the United States. They could also discuss that the likelihood of developing colon cancer increases with age, family history, and other risk factors.

The doctor could then explain the benefits of getting screened for colon cancer, such as the potential to detect and remove precancerous polyps before they turn into cancer. The doctor could also address any concerns the patient might have about the screening process, such as the discomfort associated with the procedure, by explaining that it's relatively painless and that the advantages of early detection surpass the temporary pain.

Figure 6. Protection Motivation Theory

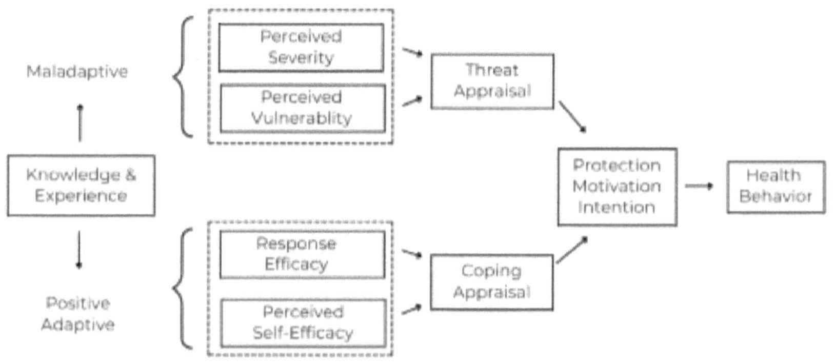

Finally, the doctor could provide resources to make it easy for the patient to get screened, such as a list of screening centers and their contact information. By using PMT to guide their communication, the doctor can help their patients understand the severity of the threat, the effectiveness of the recommended behavior, and the ease of adopting the recommended behavior, thereby increasing the likelihood that they will get screened for colon cancer.

Here are a couple of fear message examples for you to review:

The first example is a fear message about the risks of not eating healthily. "Eating unhealthy foods can lead to obesity, diabetes, heart disease, and other health problems. These conditions can greatly impact your quality of life and even shorten your lifespan. However, by making simple changes to your diet and eating more fruits and vegetables, you can greatly reduce your risk of these diseases. So don't wait until it's too late - take control of your health now and prioritize healthy eating."

The second example is a fear message about the risks of not managing stress."Chronic stress can lead to various health problems, including high blood pressure, heart disease, and depression. But there are simple steps you can take to manage stress, like practicing yoga or meditation, getting regular exercise, and setting aside time for self-care. By managing your stress, you can improve your overall health and well-being and reduce your risk of developing these serious health issues."

In both examples, the fear message is presented in a way that emphasizes the negative consequences of not taking action to protect oneself while also offering actionable steps that can be taken to mitigate those risks. The message is designed to motivate the listener to take steps to protect their health and well-being.

Final Thoughts on Models of Behavioral Change

As a natural healthcare practitioner ensuring your patients show up for their appointments, follow pro-health behaviors, adhere to treatment plans, and ultimately return to health and stay healthy are at the heart of natural medicine. Unfortunately, the conventional medical model functions more like a traditional business model, similar to what you might find at an automotive repair facility. In this model, people get sick, set up an appointment (if possible), bring their sick self or family member to a medical office, emergency room, or urgent care facility, get evaluated and maybe given a prescription, then sent home to get better, told to return in two weeks or when worse. Conversely, in natural medicine (i.e., integrative, alternative, or complementary), practitioners follow a health-based model of care focusing on preventing illness and maintaining health.

The persuasive and behavioral change models in this chapter are essential to remember to assist your patients and clients with their health goals. Understanding the frameworks and constructs, you can better know where patients may go astray. In addition, you now have the tools to intervene and be proactive in your approach.

With the inherent authority your position offers, as a doctor or natural healthcare practitioner, you're already poised to make a difference in the lives of your patients or clients. Additionally, by understanding the power of influence and behavioral change strategies, your practice will create a tremendous difference for your patients and your bottom line.

After completing the book, please re-read this section and refresh your understanding of the complexities of behavioral change and influence. Then, imagine the good you'll be able to accomplish with the information you've already gained. Moving forward, I will guide you through many topics you're probably more familiar with. Yet, there is still a lot to learn and apply. I can't wait to share it with you.

DESIGNING FOR IMPACT:
How to Transform Your Website from Drab to Fab

"Your website is the digital storefront of your business. Make it inviting and easy to navigate." - Unknown

When I was working in the wine industry, I became convinced that visitors' experiences began well before they stepped into our tasting room. The experience probably started when a friend told them about the winery and the fantastic wines we crafted. Eventually, their interest was piqued enough for them to take action. The first action was to visit our website, check us out, get a feel for who we are, and do a gut check to get a sense that the winery was a place they'd feel comfortable visiting. Especially for new wine consumers visiting a winery is a big deal, a big step, filled with excitement and trepidation. Fear of looking foolish, ignorant, and "not doing it right" is still an issue for so many winery visitors - so folks would take on at least four different coping strategies to deal with these insecurities:

1. They'd overcompensate by acting the part of the wine snob.
2. Shyly step into the tasting room, where we'd slowly guide them through the wine-tasting process.
3. Visit with an experienced friend.
4. Not visit.

Whether we're talking about winery visitors or clients/patients, it's the same story.

Generally, the same principles and process likely apply to the clients you want to attract. You're on the right path if someone is interested enough to visit your website. Their interest is piqued enough to search for your practice; maybe a friend or colleague referred them to you. They do some reconnaissance and visit your website to see if you'd be a good fit. This is where all the hard work you put in while developing your brand guide will pay dividends. These prospective clients/patients are feeling much like our winery visitors.

For example, they may feel:

1. Insecure about trying something new.
2. Unsure if you can help them.
3. Anxious about meeting a new health care provider (particularly if they have had a bad experience in the past).
4. They are naive about their body and health and are scared they may look foolish.

Because you've set a high-quality standard for your website, provided valuable content (without being too wordy - more about this later), and created a warm, welcoming, and informative site, your guests (future patients/clients) feel comfortable clicking or calling you for an appointment.

Not surprisingly: recent research suggests young adults prefer the convenience and ease of using online appointment scheduling systems over making a phone call to schedule a medical appointment. For example, a study published in the Journal of Medical Internet Research in 2018 found that among a sample of young adults aged 18-29, 72% reported a preference for online appointment scheduling. Another study published in the Journal of Medical Systems in 2019 found that among a sample of young adults aged 18-35, 80% reported a preference for online appointment scheduling.

Additionally, young adults are more likely to use the internet and technology than older adults, which may also contribute to their preference for online appointment scheduling. For example, a study published in the Journal of Medical Internet Research in 2018 found that among a sample of young adults aged 18-29, 96% reported using the web to find health information, and 68% reported using a smartphone to access health information.

Overall, research suggests that young adults prefer online appointment scheduling over making a phone call to schedule a medical appointment. Given the large proportion of young adults who use the internet and smartphones for health-related purposes, healthcare providers should consider offering online appointment scheduling to improve access and convenience for this population. While it's true that younger generations tend to prefer online booking, the universe of potential clients/patients is expansive. Many over 50 may like alternative options, such as calling to book an appointment. Bottom line: make sure you have your bases covered. Hence, all demographics feel welcome, and it's easy for anyone to book an appointment.

When you're at the point of setting up your business, one of the first steps folks think about is naming their business and building a website. The following section provides some guidance and a warning (please read that) to make your process go more smoothly.

First Things First

How often do you use an online search engine to find a service, product or get directions? Recently, our daughter-in-law asked us to help her find a new healthcare provider near her, so like most of us, we headed to our favorite search engine and typed in a few choice keywords: Naturopathic Physicians Near X Town. At first glance the results appeared encouraging, then we started to click through from the top of the list to the bottom with a wide array of results, some of which were frustrating, others discouraging, others led to deadends. So, what can you do to build a kick-ass web presence?

Don't get ahead of yourself!

The name game is one of the most important and challenging aspects of creating a business. If you already have a business name and a website, then skip ahead, but for those of us that are in the planning stages - read on.

Imagine creating a business, choosing a business name, and likewise thinking about searching for and securing a domain name for your new business. Determining what comes first - the business name or the URL - can be confusing. So here's a good path forward:

- <u>Create a List of Possible Business Names</u>: We want to love the name of our business as it's a reflection of us, our business, our brand, and how we want to be perceived; however, we also need to be prepared, as we're doing the initial name building process we need to be prepared for the fact that somebody may have already claimed our business name or our favorite URL is already snagged. Most states' Secretary of State offices (or similar) have a search engine that allows you to search to see if a business name is available; if so, snag it. Then once you have a business name, proceed to see if it is available through your favorite web-hosting site. Most website-building sites (e.g., WIX or Squarespace) also have a domain search service where you can search and, if available, secure it.

  WARNING: do not use your favorite search engine to search for potential domain names until you've secured a name for your business from your state. Why? Because URL bots track searches and are then claimed by URL bandits (that's what I'm calling them) who then snag the URL and own it - and then want to sell it to you at a high price.

Avoid searching until you have your name secured within your state.

Several years ago, before I learned better, I used an online domain finder by typing in prospective names to see if they were available. When I was ready to secure the name, one of those URL bandits purchased the domain, and I was screwed. Frustrating!

● <u>A DBA May be in Order</u>: DBA (Doing Business As) is a filing you can make with your Secretary of State Office (SoS), allowing you to do business under an assumed identity. Here's an example: you just claimed and completed your initial filing with the SoS as Johnson Natural Healthcare, LLC, and then decided to create a DBA, specifically Johnson Naturopathic Clinic. In some states, you can have multiple DBA, so imagine one day you want to build an affiliated company that creates nutritional supplements called EarthSmart Nutraceuticals - you can create another DBA. I am not a legal or tax expert, so if this is in your future, I encourage you to consult with a tax accountant and business lawyer to ensure you're making a wise financial business decision.

Before we begin our discussion about what to include on your website, I want to reflect on your end users. Throughout this book, I'll consistently return to the issue of your target audience. It makes sense, too, right? Suppose your target audience is an aging population. In that case, you'll want to ensure your fonts are appropriately sized and your messaging resonates with them. I'd encourage you to spend some time perusing several websites, both within your discipline and outside, and view them as if you were the one seeking a service. It'll put you in the right mindset and help you with your design. One of the first things I notice is that many natural health providers frequently overwhelm me with content and talk over my head. Don't make that mistake. Keep in mind whom you are talking to and their attention span.

Communication & Attention Span

Your website reflects your business personality and is likely the first contact point with prospective clients/patients and customers. Hence, it's essential to communicate in a way that captures and holds their attention. Remember also to follow the brand guide you created.

If you've received an advanced professional degree (e.g., ND, Ph.D., MD, DC, MBA), chances are you have acquired much knowledge. That's awesome; congratulations! You should be proud of yourself, seriously. You may be an educator by nature who wants to help and heal others. Your website is your welcome mat, and when folks visit, you'll want them to feel welcomed, right, not lectured or talked at - who wants that? Nobody, yet I see this all of the time with long, excessively, and painfully long lists identifying a medical textbook's worth of treatment options and modalities used in practice, then another long list of the sorts of disorders the provider specializes in. Long lists give the impression that you need to figure out what you're doing, and one cannot be an expert in everything.

"An Expert of Everything is an Expert of Nothing." ~Brad Johnson

There is a delicate balance between clearly articulating your expertise and overwhelming a potential client with a mountain of information. Would you want to visit someone who talks *at* you for 5 minutes, telling you all the fantastic things they can do in extreme detail every time you knock on their door? It's tempting when building your website to view successful practices' websites and your colleagues' pages and to model a website after theirs. We've done the same thing and came to another conclusion - to keep our sites attractive and streamlined with the essential elements designed to pique interest and elicit contact - because once a client/patient reaches out, you'll likely book them. I like to think of our website as a dance we're having with potential and current clients - all of whom have short attention spans but ultimately need our help. Let's meet them where they are.

Attention spans have decreased in recent years due to the increased use of technology and the constant bombardment of information. In the past 40 years, the average attention span has reduced from 12 seconds to 8 seconds. This has made it more challenging for written communication to capture and retain readers' attention.

To increase readership, it is vital to make the content engaging and easily digestible. You can accomplish this by using short paragraphs, bullet points, headings, and images to break up the text. Additionally, using simple and direct language can make it easier for readers to understand the content.

It's also important to consider the format of the content. For example, videos and infographics can be more engaging than text alone. Moreover, storytelling and personalization can connect with readers on a deeper level and make the content more relatable and memorable. Another way to increase readership is to optimize the content for search engines, which can yield greater visibility and reach a wider audience.

Finally, sharing content on social media can also help increase readership. We'll talk more about Content Marketing later on, first let's turn our attention to what to include in a website.

Building a Kick-Ass Web Presence

Most web hosting sites have a way to secure a URL during the purchase process, making getting a URL and a website simultaneously a simple process. It's nice to have things consolidated, and it's one less thing to keep track of once your practice starts to take off and time becomes limited. As with many marketing tasks, you can do it yourself, hire someone, or ask a friend. Friends are great, but we've already discussed some of the pitfalls of relying on friends. If determined to use the help of a friend, make sure you ultimately have access to all of the usernames and passwords for when your friend leaves town or stops helping. Okay, I'll stop preaching; you've been warned.

If you're already in business and are satisfied with the functionality and attractiveness of your website, then I'd recommend you still peruse this section; however, if you are dissatisfied or are a new owner, read on.

With so many web hosting platforms available to choose from, your choice comes down to a few key considerations:

1. Who will build and maintain the website?
2. How experienced are you with building websites?
3. What is the purpose of your website?
4. Who is your audience?

<u>Design and Maintenance of Website</u> - Many options are available for designing and maintaining a website today. You may choose an independent contractor to do the website build and lean on them for updates; you may hire a marketing firm to do all this work or do it yourself. Remember that designing and maintaining your website can be an enjoyable and creative exercise allowing you to keep complete control. As I'm fond of saying, every business owner should be able to do all the tasks their business demands. Of course, once you figure it out, you can pass off some of the jobs to employees or consultants later. Still, it's worth knowing how all the pieces of your business work - it'll save you money down the road.

<u>To Build or Not to Build</u> - If you want to build your website, consider if you have the experience, time, and knowledge to develop and grow

a website. Many website builder sites make this relatively easy, and you can create beautiful websites. It would be best to consider whether this is what you want to do with your time. If you are a doctor in private practice and are just starting, there's a good chance you'll have plenty of time to build a website, even create a nice one with a blog and other goodies. However, imagine a time when you are swamped - it's coming if you're patient. If so, what will happen to your website? Of course, at that time, you can reach out to a consultant to help or build that into your long-term plans. I've seen many dated and forgotten websites, with links that no longer work and blog pages left unattended for years. I can't think of anyone who values inattention to detail, particularly from a healthcare provider. Neglected pages with stale content sends the wrong message to your current and prospective clients.

<u>Purpose of Your Website</u> - This may seem an odd question to consider, but what is the purpose of your website? I'll answer this one for you. Your website is a crucial element of your Marketing Plan and is often the first impression a prospective client, patient, or customer gets of your business. Imagine what happens when a visitor finds a website unattractive, verbose, disconnected, and full of jargon. When I view those kinds of websites, I think of the business similarly: rambling, disorganized, and jargony. That's not what I look for in a company, in a healthcare provider - just the opposite. Therefore, I encourage my clients to think of their website as their calling card or welcome mat; we want to make our visitors feel glad they visited, get the essential information they need (without oversharing or overstating), and make it easy for them to book an appointment, purchase goods and services, or ask a question. Remember, we want to engage with our current and prospective clients.

<u>My Target Audience Is</u> - Throughout this book, I'll repeat this question, "who is your target audience?" Being clear and laser-focused about this crucial question will guide your business to success more quickly

than if you take a shotgun approach (i.e., believing everyone is your target market). Identifying your target audience will guide your website design, what to include on your website, and all of your marketing and communications; and once you've gotten clear and consistently and patiently apply the principles in this book, you'll find your business takes off. As a result, your life becomes much more enjoyable, predictable, and stress-free.

Now that we've gotten more explicit about the nuts and bolts of website design, purpose, and target audience, let's focus on what to include on your website.

What to Include on your Site

When building a website, it's tempting to view the websites of associates, friends, and colleagues with envy, thinking they've figured it out. Chances are the answer is more nuanced than we'd like to believe. Suppose you want to emulate a long-standing and thriving practice. You may be tempted to use that practice website as an exemplar, even if it is dated and excruciating verbose. Be cautious and use what works for you and toss the rest - and always keep in mind whom you're targeting and their attention span.

Before I jump into what to include in your website, I want to pause for a quick moment to remind you that about 50% of all website viewers are using a desktop computer, meaning the other half are viewing via mobile devices, so make sure your website is optimized for both desktop and mobile devices.

Okay, next, I'll outline the essential pages and topics a well-built natural healthcare business should include:

<u>Homepage</u> - This page should be an attractive, clear, and concise welcome to your page and services.

<u>About Us</u> - You'll want to include information about your qualifications, experience, and approach to natural healthcare. As with all of your communications, keep this concise and interesting. You don't need your full curriculum vitae (CV), but if you want to include that, I encourage you to keep the bio short and add a link to the full CV (add it as a PDF) .

<u>Services</u> - A concise description of the services offered, such as acupuncture, herbal medicine, nutrition, and massage therapy. Be careful not to over-explain; if you must use technical terms, it is important to translate those into everyday language. I like seeing a brief list of services that represent categories, such as "Chronic Illness," rather than an exhaustive list of nearly every chronic illness. We want to make it easy for our patients, clients, or customers to understand what we're doing without overwhelming them. We want to excite them into action and not frustrate them into inaction.

<u>Testimonials</u> - This section is a "nice-to-have" part of your website, but if you're new and don't have views or testimonials to share, it can give the wrong impression. I'd hold off adding this section until you have at least five positive reviews (and if you do use a review, make sure to get the writer's approval before using the content). Overall, positive reviews and testimonials from satisfied patients will build trust and credibility.

<u>Contact Us</u> - Always include a clear and easy-to-find contact page with the provider's address, phone number, email, and a contact form.

<u>FAQs</u> - It may be difficult to build an FAQ section before you know the kinds of questions your clients have in advance; however, we can anticipate several kinds of questions a new patient might have, such as the types of insurance accepted, payment policy, and services offered, for example.

<u>Blog</u> - With the upsurge of short-form videos on social media, it's tempting to believe blogging is dead. It isn't. As you'll learn later in the book, Content Marketing is a fantastic way to connect with your clients and prospects by providing them with useful, informative, and trustworthy news and stories. The content I post on my blogs originates from the stories I create for my monthly newsletter, then repurposed for my blogs. Integrating my content allows me to use it in many different ways. The blog is a perfect platform to share or create more robust stories that can easily be found, read, and shared. Unfortunately, many blog pages fall victim to inattention and slowly die. Maintained and Search Engine Optimized (SEO) blogs can also enhance search performance for your website, bonus! Therefore, a regularly updated blog on health and wellness topics provides valuable information to patients and can make your website more easily found.

<u>Appointment Scheduling</u> - Make it easy for your patients and clients to book an appointment with an online booking system.

<u>Patient Portal and Medicinary</u> - If you're using an electronic health record (EHR) system, then you'll want to include access to this functionality (often applied as HTML Code you add to a page); additionally, if you're contracted with an herbal/supplement company you'll want to include access to your page.

<u>Payment Options and Insurance Accepted</u> - Clients and patients will want to know if you take insurance, and if you do, which insurance you accept. If you do not accept insurance but are willing to create a " superbill," include that information. Make it easy for visitors to see your payment options and payment methods accepted, and include expectations regarding late payments and delinquent accounts.

<u>Privacy Policy and Terms of Service</u> - In healthcare, it's necessary to comply with HIPAA. According to the US Centers for Disease Control (CDC), "The Health Insurance Portability and

Accountability Act of 1996 (HIPAA) is a federal law that requires the creation of national standards to protect sensitive patient health information from being disclosed without the patient's consent or knowledge." For more, see: https://www.cdc.gov/phlp/publications/topic/hipaa.html

Here's a sample HIPAA statement:

"Protecting the privacy and security of our patients' confidential health information is of utmost importance to us. As a healthcare business, we are committed to complying with the Health Insurance Portability and Accountability Act (HIPAA) and all applicable state and federal laws governing the use and disclosure of Protected Health Information (PHI).

We maintain administrative, physical, and technical safeguards to protect the confidentiality, integrity, and availability of PHI. Our employees and contractors receive training on our HIPAA policies and procedures, and we have implemented measures to ensure that PHI is accessed only by authorized personnel for permitted purposes.

We will not disclose PHI to anyone without a valid authorization from the patient or as otherwise permitted or required by law. We will also notify our patients in the event of a breach of their unsecured PHI.

If you have any questions or concerns about our HIPAA policies and procedures, please do not hesitate to contact us."

What not to include on your site (or 5 ways to ruin a perfectly good website)

I've lost more hair in the past couple of years as a result of viewing poorly created websites, and with a fist of my hair still in hand, I offer you the Top 5 Ways to Ruin a Perfectly Good Website:

<u>Yakety Yak</u> - Whew! I've seen some websites that make me cringe, not from the overall design or aesthetics, but from an overdose of content. As a highly trained professional, your brain is filled with essential and valuable information you wish to share. You may be tempted to throw it all up on your website. Please don't. Our websites are a vital part of our Marketing Plan and serve as a teaser to get folks to book an appointment or purchase a product or service. Instead of listing every single ailment you treat or modality you use in your practice, take a beat and organize them into categories. Nobody wants to review an exhaustive list of disorders you treat; instead, using types such as Chronic Illness, Depression, and Pediatrics will suffice and ultimately lead prospects to reach out - which is what we want. If they reach out for an exploratory call, we've done our job - better yet, once they book an appointment, we're moving in the right direction.

Additionally, I know there is a good chance you're highly intelligent and very well-educated, and I expect others know that too; however, make sure you temper any desire to post a full CV on a page on your website. Many folks also strongly desire to write an extended essay illuminating their journey into their field. Those are excellent stories you can include in a blog post, newsletter, or as a linked PDF in your "about" section. There isn't any need to fill up an entire webpage with your bio, history, or resume. Again, if you feel compelled to share, I'd limit those to linked PDFs visitors must click to read. A concise biography is preferable; perhaps 2-3 short paragraphs are sufficient. When I see an overly long biography, resume, or other pieces about the author, I get the impression that they are compensating for a lack of knowledge or experience. Keep it short and engaging, and convert a reader to a client/patient.

Jargon - Please, please, please keep the professional vocabulary to an absolute minimum. Practitioners who use an overwhelming amount of jargon are building walls between the doctor and patient. Communicate clearly using everyday language. It's okay to use a medical term but then quickly explain it in everyday language; otherwise, you're likely turning off your prospects, and there's a likelihood they will look elsewhere for someone who'll speak with them, not at them. If you are professionally educated, there's a good chance you're not trying to talk over our heads. It's just that's the way you learned to communicate with your teachers and colleagues. Check yourself when communicating to ensure you're not talking over our heads or down to us. It's a delicate balance, but you're smart and want prospective patients, clients, or customers to like and trust you. You've got this!

Too Many Tabs - When building a website, you'll be challenged to keep your content concise and organized in a way that makes browsing streamlined. I've visited websites with about a dozen tabs, and under those, dozens more sub-tabs. It's easy to let your website creep out of control until your tabs and subtabs have subtabs. Stop the madness! I'm kidding, sort of. I keep returning to the purpose of a website, which is a marketing tool acts to tempt prospects into booking an appointment or purchasing a product or service - not to answer every question a visitor may have. Keep your website simple, attractive, and elegantly concise. Visitors will appreciate it, and those whose interest is piqued enough will reach out to you or book an appointment - those are the people you want.

The Long, Long List - I've literally seen websites that list dozens of ailments a practitioner treats. Don't be the one who lists all of the maladies they "specialize" in treating, like this:

1. Digestive disorders such as irritable bowel syndrome (IBS),

Crohn's disease, ulcerative colitis, and constipation.
2. Chronic fatigue syndrome (CFS) and fibromyalgia.
3. Allergies and food sensitivities.
4. Anxiety, depression, and other mood disorders.
5. Insomnia and other sleep disorders.
6. Menstrual cramps, PMS, and other menstrual disorders.
7. Menopause symptoms such as hot flashes, night sweats, and mood changes.
8. Chronic pain such as back pain, joint pain, and headaches.
9. High blood pressure and other cardiovascular conditions.
10. Diabetes and metabolic syndrome.
11. Autoimmune diseases such as rheumatoid arthritis, lupus, and multiple sclerosis.
12. Skin conditions such as eczema, psoriasis, and acne.
13. Asthma and other respiratory conditions.
14. Infertility and reproductive disorders.
15. Chronic infections such as Lyme disease and Epstein-Barr virus.
16. Thyroid disorders such as hypothyroidism and hyperthyroidism.
17. Adrenal fatigue and other hormonal imbalances.
18. Autism and other developmental disorders.
19. Cancer prevention and supportive care.
20. Heavy metal toxicity and other environmental toxin exposures.
21. Chronic sinusitis and other sinus conditions.
22. Chronic kidney disease and other kidney disorders.
23. Hepatitis and other liver disorders.
24. Candida overgrowth and other fungal infections.
25. Arthritis and other joint disorders.
26. Obesity and weight management.
27. Alzheimer's and other cognitive disorders.

28. Parkinson's and other movement disorders.
29. Multiple chemical sensitivities.
30. Post-traumatic stress disorder (PTSD) and other psychological traumas.
31. Athletic injuries and sports medicine.
32. Osteoporosis and other bone disorders.
33. Attention deficit hyperactivity disorder (ADHD) and other attention disorders.
34. Migraines and other types of headaches.
35. Chronic inflammation and other immune system disorders.
36. Chronic Lyme disease and other tick-borne illnesses.
37. Hypertension and other blood pressure disorders.
38. Insulin resistance and other metabolic disorders.
39. Chronic skin conditions such as rosacea, dermatitis, and acne.
40. Men's health issues such as prostate enlargement and low testosterone.
41. Women's health issues such as polycystic ovary syndrome (PCOS) and endometriosis.
42. Seasonal affective disorder (SAD) and other seasonal mood disorders.
43. Chemical sensitivity and other environmental sensitivities.
44. Chronic obstructive pulmonary disease (COPD) and other lung conditions.
45. Addiction and substance abuse.
46. Chronic viral infections such as hepatitis and HIV/AIDS.
47. Chronic stress and stress-related disorders.
48. Chronic pain due to injury or surgery.
49. Chronic fatigue syndrome (CFS) and myalgic encephalomyelitis (ME).
50. Gastrointestinal disorders such as acid reflux, ulcers, and inflammatory bowel disease (IBD).

Oh, sorry, did I bore you? Yep, me too, and any visitor to a website with such an exhaustive list. You're better than that, so please don't be a long list person. (Brad says: If you feel compelled to write an exhaustive list, I suggest clustering similar items under a main topic, such as Chronic Illness, and then limit your list to no more than six items). All of this illustrates a point - use the recommendations in this book, download my free Marketing Plan Guide, and work through the process. You'll be far ahead of many others. Remember, earlier in this book, I'd mentioned that "to be an expert of everything is to be an expert of nothing" - this applies here! Keep your website attractive, informative and interesting.

<u>Not Optimized for Mobile</u> - View your website on a desktop computer, laptop, tablet, Android, and iPhone. When your website is optimized, it appears consistently across any device. This is a reasonably easy fix for most web hosting platforms today.

Search engine optimization (SEO)

"SEO is no longer just about manipulating search algorithms. It's about creating content that people want and need." - Unknown

I'll be the first to say, "I am not an SEO expert," far from it. Still, I have learned much about search engine optimization and applied that knowledge to the businesses and websites I've created and managed. I encourage you to peruse the following section and apply any nuggets of wisdom to your projects. Then, if you're not getting the traction you'd hoped for, dig deeper, find books on SEO (bookstores have a ton of them), or you can hire an expert. I'm a fan of hiring an expert, particularly after I've exhausted my ability or feel the time required to learn and apply it is too time-consuming or expensive. Honestly, you can do a lot of this work yourself. Give it a try!

Understanding the Role of SEO in the Marketing Mix

Maybe you're still planning to create a practice or business, or you already have one. One of the first steps I take during the getting-ready-to-launch phase is building a website and establishing a presence on social media - it's a slow process, so hang in there. By being proactive and attentive to your target audience (yes, I'll repeatedly talk about the target audience, so if you haven't identified yours yet, it's time), you can get ahead of the SEO game by tackling some of the core issues related to getting a website found and listed high in a search.

We'll begin by looking at the low-hanging fruit. Honing your Search Engine Optimization (SEO) skills is a crucial element of your marketing plan and plays a central role in your marketing mix by helping boost your visibility and driving traffic to your website. The SEO work you'll need to accomplish begins by building quality website content structure, ensuring the site is coded appropriately to enhance its relevance, and making certain specific search terms are embedded. As I've mentioned, some of this is easily achievable by anyone with some essential website experience or done by a professional. So I'd encourage you to take a stab at it first. Below, I'll outline several of the most important tasks I encourage my coaching clients to do first:

<u>Keyword Search</u> - One of the first and easiest tasks to enhance your SEO is to conduct a keyword search using platforms like Google Keyword Planner. By identifying the most appropriate keywords and phrases for your target audience, your website will likely stand out to the right folks. The reason we care about keyword searches and phrases is that search engines scour your website and look to match search queries. Consequently, it's paramount for any website owner to ensure the website titles and meta descriptions contain relevant information so that those searching can find your business. Spending time on your keyword and relevant phrases will help you increase website traffic and drive business to you. A word of caution: avoid "keyword stuffing," as the name suggests, is an attempt to increase search visibility by filling

their pages with an inordinate number of keywords. Search engines are sophisticated and can pick up on this technique and penalize websites for this practice.

To find your website's most relevant keywords and phrases, check out Google Keyword Planner and look at Ubersuggest.

<u>Website Optimization</u> - After doing your keyword and phrase homework, you're already on the path toward optimization. You'll want to apply those keywords and phrases to your website's titles, content, meta descriptions, images, and URLs. For example, suppose you own a yoga studio in Seattle. In that case, you may want to include keywords such as "Seattle Yoga" or "Best Yoga Studio in Seattle" in your content.

Here are a few optimization tips:

- <u>Title Tags</u> - The title tag is the text that appears at the top of your browser's window and is also displayed as the main headline in search engine results. It's essential to include your target keywords in your title tag to help search engines understand what your page is about. For example, a reasonable title tag for a natural healthcare business might be "Natural Remedies and Herbal Supplements | ABC Health Clinic."

- <u>Meta descriptions</u> - A meta description summarizes your page's content that appears beneath the title tag in search engine results. It's essential to include your target keywords in your meta description to help search engines understand your pages' purpose and encourage users to click through to your website. For example, a meta description for a natural healthcare business might be "Discover the natural remedies and herbal supplements that can improve your health and wellness. Visit ABC Health Clinic today!"

Part of the optimization process is creating compelling, engaging, and valuable content for your target audience. Again, think of the end-user, the person visiting your website, and try to answer the questions you imagine they would have when visiting your site. In the same vein, it's vital to make sure your site is structurally sound. That is, ensuring your website is clear, logically organized, and easy to navigate is paramount. I can't tell you how many times I've stumbled onto a website and wondered, "what the what?"

Another crucial part of website optimization addresses the loading speed of your website. One of the ways you can improve load speed is by limiting the number of plugins you have on your site. One company I worked for had so many plugins and was so poorly optimized that it took more than 90 seconds for the page to load! We fixed that right away. A faster load time improves visitor experience and helps boost your ranking on search engines.

The final method I'll briefly discuss is using backlinks to improve your website's visibility. As the name suggests, a backlink is a link to your website from another online location. For example, when you can write a guest blog for a natural health magazine (linked back to your business), you're creating valuable information. By doing so, you're adding a sense of authority to your brand. I encourage my clients to develop social media infographics on topics they possess expert-level knowledge. Lastly, and to reiterate, creating high-quality content and building relationships with other related businesses is essential today and will serve your business well and make your website stand out.

<u>Own Your Business Listings</u> - Another approach that's easy to accomplish is to make sure your business is listed in the places where your clients or patients may search. Listing your business begins by claiming your Google Business Page (formerly known as Google My Business) and completing as much information on this page as possible

(e.g., open hours, services, insurance, images, logos, etc.). Next, I visit my Google Business Pages each week to check on reviews, make sure my information is accurate, and post updates and specials when appropriate. Creating weekly posts on your Google page helps with backlinks. Since you're already working on the Google platform, you're well on your way to increasing the likelihood of being found.

There are many other websites where you can register your business to make it easy for patients and clients to find you, as well as industry-specific "find a provider" websites. Word of caution: when I worked in the wine industry, I was trying to connect with these sorts of sites and got tangled up with a well-known hospitality reviewing site. After setting up my listing, I got a phone call from their hungry sales team, one of the dozens I'd ultimately get. I agreed to host an unofficial event at one of our tasting rooms, where a group of reviewers was to gather. The meetup was fine, and it was only afterward that the paid staff member repeatedly called, and called, and called to convince me to purchase ads from their company. That was a huge turn-off, and I mention this to let you know that many of these platforms will try to part you from your money.

Here are a couple of other platforms:

https://www.findanaturaldoctor.com/join

https://naturopathic.org/search/newsearch.asp

Be Active on Social - Another way to boost your SEO is to engage with your target audience on social media regularly. I have an entire chapter dedicated to social media and encourage you to use social judiciously and only with intent. Avoid posting when you do not have anything of value to say. I'd rather see one good post weekly than the daily chatter of meaningless drivel of rambling videos and meandering posts. I understand the attraction, and when starting a new business, it's tempting to rely overly on social media as our primary marketing tool. Don't get sucked into the "Doing Without Intention" vortex.

You're on your way now and have a good working understanding of what makes a website work well, and the basics of SEO, so let's work on a plan to get you moving forward.

MARKETING STRATEGY FOR SUCCESS:

Creating a Plan that Drives Results

"Marketing is not an event, but a process... It has a beginning, a middle, but never an end, for it is a process. You improve it, perfect it, change it, even pause it. But you never stop it completely." - Jay Conrad Levinson

If you've spent years in higher education and landed in the natural healthcare field, you may not be interested in hearing about marketing planning, strategies, or analytics. But I suspect you want to build a prosperous business or healthcare practice and earn enough money for a comfortable lifestyle. Therefore, understanding how to do marketing like a pro and making sense of analytics is essential to your success. I aim to make this process as streamlined and easy to follow as possible, avoiding unnecessary jargon and showing you the critical elements to get from here to there. Let's jump in!

Let's clarify some terms and get moving along! Marketing strategy, planning, and analytics are essential to a company's business plan. Marketing planning refers to identifying and developing marketing objectives and strategies. A marketing plan outlines a company's approach to marketing its products or services, including the tactics and resources needed to execute the plan. The Marketing Strategy activates the planning into action. It refers to the overall plan for reaching and engaging target audiences to achieve marketing goals and objectives. Marketing analytics, on the other hand, involves using data, statistical algorithms, and technology to measure, manage, and analyze marketing performance to optimize marketing effectiveness and return on investment (ROI).

Let's review some essential concepts before we dig into this section. Business goals, objectives, and strategy are related concepts crucial to any organization's success. Let's take a peek at the differences between these three terms.

<u>Business Goals</u> - Business goals are the broad, overarching aims that an organization wants to achieve. They are the desired outcomes that the organization strives for and typically define what success looks like. Business goals are often qualitative and high-level in nature. Examples of business goals include:

- Increasing revenue.

- Expanding market share.

- Improving customer satisfaction.

- Increasing brand awareness.

<u>Objectives</u> - Objectives are specific, measurable, and time-bound targets supporting business goals. They are an organization's more detailed and concrete steps to realize its goals. Objectives are often set for different needs within an organization. However, they should be aligned with the overall business goals. Examples of objectives include:

- Increasing sales by 10% in the next quarter.

- Reducing patient/client no-shows by 75% next year.

- Launching a new service by the end of the fiscal year.

<u>Strategy</u> - Strategy is an organization's plan of action to achieve its goals and objectives. It's the overall approach or roadmap that guides an organization in its decision-making and resource allocation. A business strategy typically involves:

- Identifying the organization's strengths, weaknesses, opportunities, and threats (i.e., SWOT analysis).

- Defining the target market and customer segments. Since I haven't mentioned this before, customer segmentation divides a customer base into distinct groups or segments based on specific characteristics, such as demographics, behaviors, preferences, or needs.

- Identifying our promise to our customers, also known as the value proposition.

- Determining the key activities and resources needed to deliver that value proposition.

Strategy is often a long-term plan that sets the direction for the organization and helps it stay focused on its goals.

In summary, business goals are the big-picture outcomes that an organization wants to achieve, objectives are specific targets that support those goals, and strategy is the plan of action that outlines how the organization will achieve those goals and objectives.

Success Begins with a Plan

By reading and applying the tips, tricks, and techniques in this book (and guides located on my website), you are on your way to a prosperous and thriving business. It may not feel like it right now, and that's a common feeling many of us have. But, like so many business owners or natural healthcare practitioners starting, you may feel overwhelmed, scared, and experiencing deep insecurity.

You Can Do This!

Remember when you began your training and how little you knew? The same thing applies here, and it's important to be kind to yourself as you learn new skills. However, now it's business stuff you need to know to be financially successful to survive and thrive (and pay back student loans). Many of us have severe hang-ups regarding finances, money, and charging fees for medical care. That's not lost on us; Dr. Jill and I created a coaching business to help our natural medicine friends launch and prosper without spending a fortune on unnecessary programs and broken promises.

You Have Big Skills - You're No Imposter - You Are Awesome!

You don't need additional degrees, and you don't need a specialized niche program to be the incredible practitioner you are! Don't let the insecurity vultures circle you as you stumble through practice set-up and launch. It's normal to worry that it's taking longer for your patients and clients to find you than you anticipated. Be patient and strategic.

We've Been There and Know the Way Through!

Having the right support network to help guide you through the set-up and launch, with caring and knowledgeable mentors to support you, you'll soon be on your way to prosperity. Owning your own business is one of life's biggest challenges and one of life's most fulfilling adventures.

Please take a moment, if you haven't yet, to download my Free Marketing Plan Guide right now (available at bradjohnsonmarketing.com) and begin to set the course for a successful practice or any business. Do it now, I'll wait.

Below is the outline that you'll follow when creating a marketing plan. Unless you're seeking outside funding from a bank or investors, your business plan and marketing plan are your documents - and I encourage you to be clear and concise. It's essential to refer to your plans regularly to ensure you're on the path and take corrective actions when you've deviated or lost your way. Please keep it simple and keep it functional for you!

While I encourage you to create a valuable and easy-to-follow marketing plan, it is worth the time to work through each of the elements to ensure you understand the business landscape you're entering. Of course, being hopeful and optimistic are beautiful qualities to possess, and this process is no different; however, I suggest you take a bit of a critical perspective when working on the Strength, Weakness, Opportunity, Threat (SWOT) Analysis.

Starting out can be daunting, discouraging, and frustrating for most new practitioners and new business owners when the number of patients or clients scheduled aren't meeting your expectations. Anticipate a few patients/clients initially and plan for that too (expect the first six to twelve months to be the most difficult and plan accordingly); it's the harsh reality of being your own boss. You can do this! Not to nag, but did you download the Marketing Plan guide? Great, I knew you would! You're on your way now.

Okay, scholars, let's take the plunge into the deep water where you'll fine-tune your marketing acumen, build a marketing plan and strategy and understand how you can apply marketing analytics to target your audience and grow your business.

The Marketing Plan

"Your Marketing Plan is Your Compass" ~Brad Johnson.

A marketing plan is a strategic document that outlines a business's actions to promote and sell its products or services. It typically includes market research, a SWOT analysis (strengths, weaknesses, opportunities, and threats), goals and objectives, target audience, budget, and tactics. Remember that your marketing plan is your working document, so it only needs to work for you.

Executive Summary - This is a brief overview of the marketing plan, including the product, target market, and primary goals and objectives. This section is a starting point to get you thinking like a marketing professional. There is no need to strive for perfection in this process; have fun, then be creative once you've gone through the complete Marketing Plan guide (available at bradjohnsonmarketing.com), and take another stab. If you've gone through the guide, please review this section before moving on to the analytics section.

To get you in the right frame of mind, answer the following questions using everyday language and be concise.

- Mission - What is the purpose of your business/practice, and whom do you serve?

- Vision - What are the long-term desires or guiding principles of your business?

- The Service - What services do you offer (keep it concise)?

- The Leadership - What are your leadership superpowers?

- The Overall Industry - What is the current state of your industry in your area?

- The Competitors - Who are your direct competition (those doing what you do) in your area?

- Financial Status - What is the status of your finances? Describe your start-up funds and how you'll pay for everything in detail.

- Future Plans - Where do you see your practice in five years? Outline your five-year plan (immediate through year 5)

<u>Market Research</u> - Earlier in my career, I worked as an analyst for a Marketing Research company in Seattle, conducting all sorts of research projects for business and governmental agencies. Hiring a market research firm for a small start-up business is probably beyond your budget and isn't necessary. However, we can do a lot of this work ourselves. The Market Research section outlines information about your target market, including demographics, needs, preferences, and behaviors. It may also include information about the competition.

<u>SWOT Analysis</u> - Evaluating your position within the marketplace is a necessary process. SWOT analysis evaluates the internal and external environment, highlighting Strengths, Weaknesses, Opportunities, and Threats. I always encourage my students or clients to be as critical as possible during this stage because it is necessary to be optimistic; however, it's equally vital to be critical.

<u>Goals and Objectives</u> - This section outlines the goals the company hopes to achieve with the marketing program, such as boosting the brand or increasing sales. It also includes specific objectives to help the company track progress toward these goals.

<u>Target Audience</u> - This section defines the specific group of people that the marketing campaign is targeting. Research your target by considering such factors as the general demographics information, motivation, interests, and purchasing behaviors.

<u>Budget</u> - This section outlines the financial resources allocated to the marketing campaign, including advertising, promotion, and other expenses.

<u>Tactics</u> - This section includes the specific actions that will be taken to execute the marketing plan, such as social media campaigns, email marketing, events, and content marketing. It should include details about the channels and tactics that will be used, as well as timelines and key performance indicators (KPIs) that will be used to measure success.

When you download my free Marketing Plan Guide at www.bradjohnsonmarketing.com, you'll receive a workbook that'll make it simple to get your marketing plan off the ground fast, plus you'll get the Marketing Task Sheet - a step-by-step guide to doing marketing (See example below) to put you on the right track.

Let's Not Get Ahead of Ourselves

If a Marketing Plan is your compass, the strategy is your roadmap. Likewise, if we are planning a road trip from Seattle to Colorado, we will notice mileposts along the way. Each milepost is a marker indicating the specific distance we have traveled on the route. You must first pass through each milepost along the way before jumping ahead to the end. Similarly, many new practitioners operate without much of a plan at all, jumping ahead to advanced areas before they've mastered the essential elements of their plan. Building your practice/business from the ground up is essential, honing your business/practice and marketing skills from beginner topics and, as your business grows, slowly progressing to more advanced topics. You'll gain more knowledge and skill and become an expert on your journey.

I bring this up here and in other sections because I frequently witness new practice owners struggling to find patients and clients and losing focus (probably because they have not developed their Marketing Plan) and hopping from one radical approach to the next without first nailing down the fundamentals. In my Marketing Plan guide, I provide a Marketing Task sheet where I suggest a stepwise plan forward. As in the road trip analogy, your marketing trip needs to follow a process where you slowly build your practice, learning and fine-tuning your skills, then applying the marketing principles I outline in this book step-by-step. I strongly believe that in order to be an "expert," - regardless of your degree, you should be in your field for about ten years.

So, if you are a new practitioner, just out of college or recently graduated, I strongly encourage you to put in the work to grow your practice and knowledge (that includes hitting the pause button on starting a program, which seems to be all the rage among new graduates these days). Resist the temptation to jump ahead. Instead, focus on the fundamentals: practice, learn by doing, learn from mentors or colleagues, apply the basic marketing practices first, then slowly add to your marketing repertoire over time. Soon, you'll have a thriving practice, and you will be the expert you'd hoped to become earlier in your career. Then, and only then, branch out and expand to your heart's content.

With an example, let's explore the marketing strategy of a fictitious yoga business.

Marketing Strategy

As you may recall, a marketing strategy puts all your planning into action. It refers to the overall plan for reaching and engaging target audiences to achieve marketing goals and objectives.

Here's a process you can follow when developing your marketing strategy, this one is for a made-up yoga business:

1. <u>Define the Target Audience</u> - This concept is so important that I'll keep referring to it throughout this book. I'd encourage you to take this seriously and spend whatever time you need to identify your people. You'll want to identify the

ideal customer for your yoga business. This may include demographics like age, gender, income, interests, and location.

2. <u>Develop a Brand Identity</u> - We spent an entire chapter discussing the need to brand your company properly. So, refer back to your brand guide and create a remarkable and recognizable brand that reflects the values and philosophy of your yoga business. At a minimum, this will include a logo, color scheme, and brand messaging.

3. <u>Create a Website</u> - Develop a website that showcases your yoga business and its offerings. The website should be attractive, easy to navigate, and provide essential information about the yoga classes, instructors, schedules, pricing, and location.

4. <u>Offer Promotions</u> - Offer promotional discounts, such as a free class or discounted first month, to attract new customers. Discounts can be shared through social media, email campaigns, and word of mouth.

5. <u>Use Social Media</u> - Create a strong presence on channels like Facebook, Instagram, TicTok and Twitter to promote your yoga business and engage with customers. Share updates about new classes, special events, and motivational quotes.

6. <u>Host Events</u> - Host workshops, retreats, or charity events to create a sense of community and attract new customers. Partner with local businesses to co-host events and cross-promote each other.

7. <u>Collaborate with Influencers</u> - Collaborate with influencers or bloggers in the health and wellness space to promote the yoga business to their followers.

8. <u>Collect Client/Patient Reviews</u> - Encourage clients to leave reviews on the website and social media platforms. Positive reviews can attract new patients and build trust in the brand.

9. <u>Offer Loyalty Programs</u> - Implement a loyalty program to reward clients for their continued business. This can include discounts on programs, special treatments or products.

By implementing these strategies, a yoga business can increase its visibility and attract new customers while building a loyal customer base.

Your marketing plan must be coherent in the strategies, processes, and communications used to accomplish your goals. In Holistic Marketing, communications and marketing go hand-in-hand, and integrating these concepts is at the heart of Integrated Marketing Communications (IMC).

The following sections will introduce you to the idea, explore how it fits into the marketing mix, and provide some examples to help you better understand IMC.

Integrated Marketing Communication

"IMC is the practice of unifying all marketing communications efforts so they work together and reinforce one another, making them more effective in reaching and influencing target audiences." - Lisa Nirell.

In natural healthcare, we frequently hear about integrative medicine, which espouses integrating various healing modalities to help patients improve health. The path to healing is often complex and requires the willingness and ability to use the methods to aid recovery, even if that means referring your patient to another provider. For example, suppose you are a naturopathic doctor with a patient experiencing lower abdominal pain. In that case, you may refer them for imaging. This initial referral may suggest a more significant problem requiring you to refer to a conventional medical specialist or a surgeon. Following surgery, you resume care and treatment with the full complement of naturopathic medicine, such as traditional herbal and homeopathic remedies, and incorporate visceral manipulation to help alleviate the adhesions that later develop. As an integrative practitioner, you understand the value of working together as a team.

In Integrated Marketing Communications (IMC), we follow this same holistic approach in your marketing communications. As a result, your overall marketing will improve, your workload will be moderated, and your messaging will become consistent and coherent across all channels.

IMC in the Marketing Mix

I'd been practicing an integrated marketing approach years before I understood that Integrated Marketing Communications (IMC) was a thing. In practice, it made common sense to think holistically and to work as efficiently and effectively as I could. In addition, I've always preferred to be a solo entrepreneur, so creating a way to get the biggest bang for my time and energy always seemed attractive and necessary.

In most marketing textbooks, you'll learn all about the marketing mix. The Marketing Mix (aka 4Ps of Marketing) is a set of tools designed to help us sell and promote products and services. They include Product, Price, Promotion, and Place. This view of marketing offers a simplified way to consider positioning your services or products in the marketplace. So let's take a quick peek at the 4Ps:

<u>Product</u> - The initial "P" in the Marketing Mix is a product, physical or intangible product or service being sold. It includes the product's design, features, packaging, and branding. Companies must ensure that their products/services meet the needs and wants of their target customers.

<u>Price</u> - The second "P" in the Marketing Mix is Price and refers to the amount people are willing to pay for the product. Companies must set

a competitive, profitable price that aligns with their target customers' perceived value of the product.

<u>Promotion</u> - The third "P" is Promotion which is the method used to communicate with and persuade potential customers to purchase the product. This includes advertising, personal selling, sales promotion, public relations, and direct marketing.

<u>Place</u> - The final "P" in the Marketing Mix is Place which refers to the channels used to distribute the product to the target customers. If your business sells services instead of products, think of the final "P" as the place (or area) where you will advertise or market your services. If you're selling a product, it includes distribution channels, logistics, and inventory management. Companies must ensure that their products are available in just the right place at the right time to meet their customers' needs.

The 4Ps of the Marketing Mix is a simple set of tools designed to help position your business in the marketplace. Keeping the 4Ps in mind, the IMC approach allows us to combine our marketing.

Integrated Marketing Communications is a holistic approach to marketing that seeks to seamlessly integrate all marketing communications consistently and cohesively to reach and engage customers effectively. IMC plays a key role in the marketing mix by ensuring that all marketing messages and tactics are aligned with the overall marketing strategy and objectives. This includes everything from advertising and public relations to sales promotion and direct marketing, as well as social media, digital marketing, and experiential marketing. By coordinating all these elements, IMC helps create a cohesive and consistent brand image and enables you to effectively communicate the value of your products and services to your target audience.

Developing an IMC Strategy

Integrated Marketing Communications (IMC) is a deliberate marketing approach combining various marketing communication forms (such as digital and traditional advertising, sales pitches, public relations, direct marketing, social media, and more) to deliver a consistent message to consumers. An IMC strategy coordinates all these marketing efforts to ensure that all messaging and communications are consistent across all channels.

First, I'll elaborate on the elements typically included and an IMC strategy, followed by ways to measure its effectiveness, then offer an example of an IMC strategy. All the planning approaches I present in this book are intended to help your business grow and prosper. It all begins with working through your Marketing Plan process (free marketing plan guide available at www.bradjohnsonmarketing.com), building out your Brand Guide, and dialing in how to reach your target audience (nail this down sooner rather than later).

Now we turn our attention to the worthwhile elements to include in your IMC strategy:

1. <u>Define your Target Audience</u> - Each business has a specific group of individuals that mesh well with its mission. Identifying whom you want to reach will save time and money in marketing and advertising efforts.
2. <u>Develop Straightforward Goals and Objectives</u> - By setting clear goals of what you want to achieve with your IMC program and establishing objectives, and the steps to get to your goals, you'll be setting your business up for success.
3. <u>Develop a Consistent Brand Identity</u> - Creating a brand guide, as discussed earlier, will ensure that all of your marketing materials, including your website, social media, and advertising, have a cohesive look and feel.

4. <u>Create a Budget and Allocate Resources</u> - Many businesses are set up on a shoestring budget, meaning you don't have much working-capital to spend on marketing and advertising. Therefore, determine how much you can spend on your IMC efforts and allocate resources accordingly.

5. <u>Plan and Execute your IMC Campaigns</u> - Design a process to reach your target audience and run your campaigns.

6. <u>Monitor and Evaluate your Results</u> - It's always a challenge to determine whether your actions are working. I'd encourage you to use tools such as Google Analytics and customer feedback to track the effectiveness of your IMC efforts and make adjustments as needed.

An Integrated Marketing strategy should be a solid part of your overall marketing plan, which guides how your marketing, communications, and public relations all function together.

IMC Strategy Example

We now have a good conceptualization of what is typically included in your integrated marketing plan; we'll turn our attention to an example of an IMC strategy for a fictional acupuncture business called "True Point":

1. <u>Identify the Target Audience</u> - True Point's target audience is health-conscious adults between 30 and 65. Our target market is adults who are interested in natural and holistic health solutions, including but not limited to:
   a. Individuals who are looking for alternative treatments to traditional Western medicine
   b. Health-conscious individuals who prioritize preventative care
   c. Individuals who are interested in using natural

approaches for common ailments.

2. <u>Determine the Marketing Mix</u> - True Point will use a combination of advertising (e.g., TV commercials, radio ads, online ads), sales promotion (e.g., discounts, coupons), public relations (e.g., press releases, media relations), direct marketing (e.g., email marketing, direct mail), and social media (e.g., Instagram, Facebook, Twitter) to reach its target audience.

3. <u>Set marketing goals</u> - True Point's marketing goals include increasing brand awareness, driving traffic to its storefront, and increasing sales.

4. <u>Develop the IMC message</u> - True Point's IMC message will focus on the health benefits of its acupuncture programs and the convenience of dropping in for an unscheduled "Poke and Go" treatment.

5. <u>Create a Budget</u> - True Point will allocate a budget of $5,000 for its IMC efforts for a six month campaign.

6. <u>Implement the IMC Plan</u> - True Point will launch a commercial radio campaign, run a social media promotion offering a free 15-minute exploratory call and a $50 first visit for the first 100 clients who mention the offer, and a direct mail campaign sent to local residents.

7. <u>Measure and Evaluate the Results</u> - True Point will track the success of its IMC efforts by monitoring metrics such as website traffic, social media engagement, and sales data. It will then use this information to adjust its IMC plan to meet its marketing goals.

Again, I want to underscore the value of creating plans and strategies that work for you regarding set-up, application, and evaluation. There isn't any sense in making complex plans you'll never use; instead, I encourage you to create all your plans as simply as possible. As you begin your planning processes, there will likely be times when you're unsure, such as identifying your target audience, and that's fine. This topic, in particular, tends to lock up many business owners and practitioners at the beginning of their planning process. I strongly urge you to dial in your target audience (or any other sticking point) before you launch into the planning process - it'll help you focus on everything that follows, such as your website, promotional and marketing materials, and advertisements.

Once you have an IMC strategy, launched a marketing effort, and spent some hard-earned money, you'll want to understand whether it was worth it. There are several ways a business can measure the effectiveness of its IMC program. To assess the efficacy of your efforts, you may want to track the following:

- <u>Sales</u> - Did your IMC efforts result in increased sales? Track before and after sales data.

- <u>Traffic</u> - Did your IMC efforts drive more traffic to your website or physical store? Keep pre/post records of your website and in-person traffic to determine whether your efforts are paying off.

- <u>Engagement</u> - Did your IMC efforts increase engagement on social media or other channels? You'll know if your posting is successful by monitoring your social media post engagement in terms of likes, comments, and shares.

- <u>Brand Awareness</u> - Did your IMC efforts increase awareness of your brand? This is more challenging to assess but is achievable. For example, a more significant business could hire a market research firm to explore this (expensive). Alternatively, include a survey in your email newsletter (less expensive). SurveyMonkey is an easy online tool to use for survey research.

- <u>Customer Loyalty</u> - Did your IMC efforts result in increased customer loyalty? Here are two simple ways to assess commitment: customer retention and satisfaction. Customer retention can be determined by reviewing how many customers return or never return to your business. A business owner can calculate the customer attrition rate by taking the number of clients lost within a specific timeframe, then dividing it by the total number of clients at the beginning of the timeframe. Customer satisfaction can be determined using survey research and asking clients this question: "Overall, how satisfied are you with the care you receive from us?" An easy way to do this is to ask your clients to anonymously fill out a written form on-site or via an online survey tool. Anonymity is essential if you want to get an accurate reading; that's where online surveys help.

Integrated Marketing Communications is at the heart of holistic marketing. Before we leave this chapter, I want to explore a few of the techniques used in determining the effectiveness of your marketing efforts. Using marketing analytics as a tool to assess campaign efficacy will ensure your messages are hitting the target and conversion costs.

Marketing Analytics

A good working knowledge of marketing analytics will help you better understand whether your messaging is hitting its target. I've seen how marketing analytics has leaped to the forefront of marketing in the past couple of decades, almost to the exclusion of everything else. Digital media allows almost any data-driven person to geek out into a blissed-out, analytic fugue state, waking up in a pool of drool mumbling about chi-square, regression analysis, and customer segmentation, not knowing how they got there. I say this facetiously, kind of. It's easy to go down the rabbit hole of data analytics and lose sight of our goal of connecting with clients, building relationships, and generating revenue. Don't get me wrong; data analytics is a very useful tool in helping to understand whether we are on target, understanding if our advertising is worth the money spent, and if our social media is reaching the people we hope it does.

Let's jump into it now. Marketing analytics uses data analysis and statistical methods to evaluate and optimize marketing strategies and campaigns. It involves collecting, measuring, and analyzing various types of data related to customer behavior, preferences, and interactions with a brand or product. The insights gained from marketing analytics can help you make educated decisions about your marketing approaches, such as what types of campaigns to run, where to target their advertising, and how to optimize their messaging.

Here are some examples of marketing analytics:

<u>Customer Segmentation</u> - By grouping customers into segments (or groups) based on demographics, behaviors, or purchase history, we will be better positioned to tailor our messages to this audience and improve the overall performance of a marketing campaign.

<u>Conversion Rate Optimization</u> - Simply stated, a conversion happens when the subject of a marketing message takes a desired action. Imagine you've created a Google Ad, and the messaging encourages prospective patients to sign-up for a free consultation. After the ad has been running for a while, you analyze the website data to evaluate the success of the advertisement. The data suggests visitors are making it to your website, spending a decent amount of time, but drop off before the conversion. At this point, you can review your advertising copy and

the ease with which people can navigate your website to improve the conversion rate.

A/B Testing - Fine-tuning marketing messages and testing out alternative messages side-by-side is essential to improve the quality of your campaign and performance. Also known as split testing, A/B Testing uses two variations of a marketing message and evaluates which is working better. Once a business identifies the best message, they remove the poor performer, replace it with another one, and run those to determine which is better. This ongoing process will yield the best-performing campaign.

Return on Investment (ROI) Analysis - One of the biggest challenges is determining the ROI of a marketing campaign. Just because ROI can be difficult to ascertain sometimes, that doesn't mean we should shy away from trying to understand the ROI of a campaign only to let you know it's more complicated than one might imagine. The idea is that we compare the costs of the campaign versus the revenue generated from the campaign. It's complicated to assess ROI because a marketing campaign generally isn't operating in a vacuum. That is to say, we may be promoting something particularly special, but our other marketing tools (e.g., website, social, etc.) are still operating and in effect. Therefore, I encourage my clients to keep track of the analytics related to each marketing project in operation, track visitors to their website, account for foot traffic to their business, and always (always) ask a client, patient, or customer how they found out about your business.

Social Media Analytics - Social media platforms make analyzing the performance of marketing messages and advertising campaigns easy. Take time each week to evaluate the success of your social media posts (remember to try A/B testing) and begin to hone in on the specific messaging and visual content to determine what's working best and what's flopping. Review the engagement of your posts, likes, follows, and shares, and review the demographics, as it'll help you improve the performance of your social media messaging.

Final Words about Planning & Analytics

I've known people who've created basic business plans on the back of a napkin and have successfully flown by the seat of their marketing pants while growing their businesses. For whatever reason, some folks have a knack for launching businesses; I hope you're one of them. But, if you're like the rest of us, having a plan to guide us forward is essential to our business's smooth growth and operation. For the most part, there isn't a need to hire a marketing consulting firm and create a hardbound exhaustive business and marketing plan (unless you want to secure significant funding from a bank or a venture capitalist - that's another story). Still, for the majority of us, we need an excellent plan to get our business off the ground, a marketing plan and strategy to guide us to success, as well as a way to evaluate our progress along the way; that's the utility of analytics.

As you've likely gathered by now, I'm an advocate of doing it myself, and this DIY philosophy is etched in my DNA. All small business owners should know how to do it themselves. Once you've got a handle on the essential functions of your business and growth is moving in a positive direction, then it's more practical to farm out the workload to staff or subject matter consultants.

THE POWER OF SOCIAL:

Leveraging Social Media for Brand Awareness & Engagement

"Social media is not a one-way megaphone, it's a conversation." - Amy Jo Martin

Spend a few minutes reviewing business content on social media, and I'll bet you come to the same conclusion: social media is filled with a tremendous amount of 1-way communication. I think of these folks as "broadcasters," much like a radio station whose signal radiates in all directions. Nobody can talk back - without calling the station. These broadcasting communicators speak at you, not with you - you probably know a few folks like this. We know from earlier in the book that good communication requires these six fundamental components: active listening, mutual respect, open-mindedness, clear communication, empathy, and authenticity.

I'd encourage you to remember the six elements of good communication every time you speak, share verbal or written communication, and practice listening more than talking.

Browse the shelves of almost any bookstore, and chances are you'll find entire books dedicated to this single topic: social media. While my intention isn't to offer a comprehensive overview of social media, I wish to share many of my experiences working in this sphere for almost two decades and minimize the time you need to spend on social media in your marketing plan.

The Changing Face of Social Media

Social media constantly evolves, with new platforms and features always emerging. Currently, some of the most popular social media platforms include Facebook, Instagram, Twitter, TikTok, and LinkedIn; however, by the time you read this, some of these may have faded in prominence or dissolved, or other new replacements have taken their space. Nevertheless, billions worldwide use these platforms to connect with friends and family, share information and media, and stay informed about what's happening in the neighborhood and worldwide.

Let's look over the horizon into the future. First, we will likely see continued growth and innovation in the social media space. Some potential trends include an increased focus on privacy and security, the rise of more niche and specialized platforms, and the integration of artificial intelligence and virtual reality into the social media experience. Additionally, social media usage will likely continue to increase as more people worldwide gain access to the internet and smartphones.

There will likely also be a push for more regulation and monitoring of social media content by government and private organizations to curb the spread of misinformation and hate speech. Additionally, there may be more pressure on social media companies to take more responsibility for moderating their platforms and protecting users' data.

In my introduction section, I elaborated on the concepts of the Copy-Paste Mentality and Doing Without Intention. This is a good time to go back and review those concepts if you skipped that section. While social media is a significant marketing tool for anyone trying to get noticed, grow their business, and build community connections. It can also be a tremendous waste of time as it gives you the impression that you're doing marketing. As an early adopter of social media, as a way to build community and get the word out, I quickly jumped on with MySpace, and started playing in the Facebook world in 2005. I saw the potential value of building connections and community using these nascent platforms. I first used them to help wrangle my graduate student friends to go out for drinks, and later as a professional marketer, tempting wine enthusiasts to visit the winery where I was working.

Many businesses at that time were wary of these new online platforms believing they were a fad or simply a waste of time. "They'd say "that's where the kids were playing, and not where *real* customers gather," I recall having to coax the owners of a winery to allow me to establish a presence on social media, first with Facebook, and after it became clear we were far ahead of other competing wineries, gaining new fans, we added new platforms. In those early days before the platforms exploded and monetized everything through a near-constant stream of advertisements, a time when you could connect with people and view their feeds, comment and interact was a heady time - kind of like Woodstock without the good music, sex, and drugs. We grew our presence from a few folks to a few thousand followers quickly and easily - ah, the good old days! Alas, fast-forward to 2023, the feeds are clogged with paid promotions and very little content from my friends, neighbors, or industry pals.

The current landscape of social media is characterized by constant flux and complexity, where trends and algorithms are ever-changing. Yet, despite its challenges and flaws, it remains a crucial space we must recognize.

What Does the Data Suggest

Let's turn our attention to a trusted source of information about what's happening in the social media sphere, The Pew organization. The Pew

Research Center is *"a nonpartisan fact tank that informs the public about the issues, attitudes and trends shaping the world." (Pew Website.)*

In 2005, the Pew Research Center began tracking social media when only about 5% of US adults were using at least one of the social media platforms. Six years later, in 2011, more than half of all Americans were active on social media, and at the time of their 2021 report, 72% of the American public used some social media source.

While social media platform preferences shift, our tastes change by age and gender. We learned from Pew in 2021 that about 69% of social media users engage with Facebook - still the most powerful platform (women: 77% and men: 61%) with minimal variation between those aged 18-64 (averaging around 75%) while approximately 50% over 65 years old are using Facebook. Slight variation between race, income, and education exists for Facebook users. However, Instagram is far from Facebook's power, with around 40% of social media users on this platform. Instagram users tend to bias toward younger generations, with those aged between 18-29 appearing to be the most active (approximately 71%), and the percentages drop off as the age increases. Forty-eight percent of 30-49-year-olds use Instagram, while less than 30% of 50-64-year-olds use it, dropping to around 13% for those over 65. Similar patterns related to age and gender exist for Instagram users. However, there were significant differences between white folks and people of color and use of the platform (e.g., whites: 35%, black: 49%, and hispanic:52%) as well as between urban/suburban and those living in rural areas (45, 41, 25% respectively).

At the time of this 2021 report, only 21% indicated they used TicTok. According to the January 2023 report from Comscore, usage of TicTok by Americans was broken down by age group, such that those aged 10-19 accounted for 32.5% of users; those 20-29 – 29.5%, 30-39 – 16.4%, 40-49 – 13.9%, 50+ – 7.1%. Data suggests additional older users are joining the platform; however, 78.4% of all TicTok users are under 40.

The next groupings of social media platforms need to catch up to Facebook and Instagram. The report indicates "X." formerly Twitter, with 23%, Pinterest with 31%, and Snapchat with 25%. With the 2022 purchase of Twitter by Elon Musk, time will tell how this platform will fare.

81% of users indicate they use YouTube, with the data skewing towards the younger generations. Only 49% of users aged 65+, compared to 95% of users aged 18-29, engage with the video platform. An eighty-one percent is a significant number of users. As you progress with your marketing, consider engaging with this platform (more about video marketing later).

So, how often do Americans use social media? The 2021 Pew study also looked into the frequency of use, finding the following:

- Facebook - Daily: 70%, Weekly: 17%, Less Frequently: 12%

- Instagram - Daily: 59%, Weekly: 21%, Less Frequently: 20%

- Snapchat - Daily: 59%, Weekly: 21%, Less Frequently: 19%

- YouTube - Daily: 54%, Weekly: 29%, Less Frequently: 16%

- Twitter - Daily: 46%, Weekly: 27%, Less Frequently: 27%

This data reinforces what we probably intuitively knew already - many people engage with social media daily!

How about Podcasts? Social media is also quickly becoming a news source, particularly for those under 29. According to a July 2021 Pew Research Center survey, about a quarter (23%) of U.S. adults sometimes get news from podcasts. That's a worrying statistic, particularly for those in the healthcare industry. While many podcasters are subject matter experts, an exceptionally large number are opinion-based shows whose "knowledge" may incorrectly inform their followers. Regarding health-related podcast programming, it's "listener-beware" - be wary of charismatic broadcasters. And, for those who enjoy sharing natural health knowledge, you may want to consider creating your pwn podcast (more about that in the Digital Media chapter).

Social Media Marketing

Social media is ubiquitous and essential in building relationships with prospective and current clients. Social media marketing is a form of digital marketing using social media platforms to promote businesses, products, or services. It can include creating and sharing content, running social media ads, and engaging with customers on social media. Social media marketing can play several roles in the marketing mix.

Over the years, I have successfully used social media marketing as an effective way to increase brand awareness for the companies I've worked for and owned. Using social media platforms allows you to reach a large audience relatively quickly and with ease. Integrating and aligning your social media messaging with your mission statement and brand guide styles can help build brand recognition reaching those likely to be interested in your services. This works well when you tailor your messaging to your audience, your target audience, and the folks who want to come to your business, clinic, or practice. Make sure when creating your content to use content that encourages engagement. Let me say that again: our goal is to engage with our audience, to create space for conversation, to build credibility, to enhance trustworthiness - and that means your postings need to reflect that.

An example from early in my marketing career is not related to building practice, but the principles can still be applied. Our problem: we had a 13-acre vineyard, and our usual contracted harvest team told us, on short notice, they wouldn't be able to pick this year - 13 acres of grapes means we had to harvest about 65 tons of fresh fruit in a brief period. Crisis! We had to make a quick decision to either try to find a local team of grape pickers to hire or figure out another way to get the grapes harvested. I thought, what if we used this crisis and turned it to our advantage to engage with our customers significantly? So, I proposed we create a special event and use social media heavily to recruit four hundred volunteers to help us pick our grapes. During a typical season, we'd normally have to pay for the harvest folks to pick, so why not use that money and create a memorable experience for these volunteers?

Over four weekends in late August into early September, we welcomed the teams of volunteers (e.g., families, friends, and work colleagues) to our vineyard at dawn - early on a Saturday! With the dew on the ground and the sun rising, we'd give a briefing about how to pick the grapes over a megaphone and guide the volunteers into the vineyard, providing gloves, harvesting tools, and buckets. While they were busy picking and chatting, we'd walk through the vineyards and chat with the volunteers, talk about the grapes and winemaking in general, and the people **loved it**! Incredibly, each Saturday, they harvested quickly without any problems, and after picking, our volunteers returned to our winery for a grape stomp, a bottle of wine, a t-shirt, and lunch! The event was a tremendous community-building experience; we called it: "iPick - iStomp - iDrink!" It was a lot of work and fun, and those volunteers became lifelong fans, boosters, and some of our best customers!

How could you apply the same principle in your practice, clinic, or business? People are looking for the community; you could become the person or company that unites them. I'd love to know about your successes using innovative approaches to build community through outreach - drop me a success note at www.bradjohnsonmarketing.com

Incorporating Social Media into your Marketing Plan

Social media marketing is a crucial component of the overall marketing plan for most businesses and those who practice in the natural healthcare profession. It allows the practitioner to connect with a broader audience, increase brand awareness, and build a community of loyal patients and followers who may become your patients one day. Practitioners can use platforms such as Facebook, Instagram, and Twitter to share informative content, promote events and special offers, and engage patients. Additionally, social media can be used to gather patient feedback and reviews, which can be used to improve the practice and attract new patients. Social media can also be used to drive website traffic, which can be used to convert leads into patients. Social media marketing is a cost-effective and efficient way for a natural healthcare practitioner to reach and engage with patients.

Using social media should be a significant component of any marketing plan, offering your business several benefits:

1. <u>Targeting Specific Audiences</u> - Social media platforms offer advanced targeting options, which allow businesses to reach certain demographic groups, locations, and interest areas.
2. <u>Measuring and Analyzing Results</u> - Social media platforms provide businesses with a wealth of data on their customers and marketing campaigns, which can be used to measure and analyze the results of marketing efforts and make data-driven decisions.
3. <u>Cost-Effectiveness</u> - Compared to traditional marketing

channels, social media marketing is relatively inexpensive, which can help companies find and reach their target without spending too much money in the process.

4.

Using Social Media Effectively

Social media began as a place to connect with our friends and family. They quickly evolved (or devolved) into their current state as an advertising platform for businesses, organizations, and causes. Scroll through almost any social media channel, and chances are you'll see cute kitty videos, videos of people playing games, the periodic picture from an old friend, and loads of promotional pitches, videos, and static ads. The social media landscape is increasingly and annoyingly becoming monetized, and sponsored advertisements take significant work to avoid. So, how does a business use social media effectively and get above the background noise?

Social media can effectively grow a business if used strategically and consistently. However, the effectiveness of social media depends on interconnected factors such as the target audience, type of business, and the quality of content posted. Therefore, each company has to decide whether social media is worth it.

Let's look at an important concept and question: How does a small business determine the return-on-investment (ROI) of using social media as a marketing tool? Frankly, unless you have a large marketing department that spends considerable financial and statistical resources, it will be challenging to determine the ROI of a social media program, but that doesn't mean we shouldn't do it. Conversely, it's easier to determine ROI for social media advertising campaigns; however, we may need contributing factors that lead a prospective customer to become a customer or make a purchase. Data is handy, and data is essential, to a point. In holistic marketing, thinking of the big picture rather than the individual pieces of your marketing puzzle is necessary. You see, it's rare that anyone makes a purchase decision based upon a single encounter with any content or advertisement. We'll talk more about that later. In the meantime, our decision-making path is circuitous. Let's get back to another important topic related to the effectiveness of utilizing social media.

What is the impact of post quality and quantity? Ultimately, the question a business owner should be most concerned about is, "to what extent does social media posting lead to visits, purchases, new or returning customers, clients, or patients?" Because content creation, design development, posting, and administering a channel take a lot of time, and if you are still looking for positive results, you must ask yourself what's the point. I've said it before, and it's worth repeating: avoid the temptation of "Doing" and instead practice "Doing with Intention." In other words, post thoughtful, interesting, and engaging posts - and if your creativity is waning, take a break and return when your mojo returns. There are many other productive tasks you can work on that can drive traffic to your business. So don't get caught in the hypnotic social media "Doing" trap!

Quality and Quantity of Social Media Postings

It's not surprising that both the quality and quantity of postings can affect the outcome of your social media program. The quality and amount of social media posts can influence consumer behavior to purchase or schedule an appointment by creating a positive brand image, providing valuable information, and building trust and engagement with your target audience. Without engagement, you're simply broadcasting (and you don't want to be the talking head who goes "blah, blah, blah") - and you probably know this: 1-way communication is off-putting and moves you away from your goal of building community. Engage. Engage. Engage.

What does a high-quality post look like? High-quality posts are visually appealing, relevant, and often educational, and when perfected, you'll be able to attract and retain a large following. In addition, these sorts of high-quality posts can help establish your brand as an authority, build customer connections, and increase the chances of someone taking a behavioral action (e.g., making a purchase, visiting your website, scheduling an appointment). Finally, I'd recommend before you begin "educating" folks using social media to think twice about it. I've seen this done well and have witnessed cringe-worthy examples (don't worry, I've done both), and I encourage you to learn from my successes and failures. I am confident you are brilliant and knowledgeable about your particular training area, and it's great that you want to help educate us. However, there is a fine line between building a relationship and providing helpful information and "educating us," - relationship building is a 2-way process where you engage in a conversation with your followers, asking and answering questions. You can also anticipate the needs of your social media followers by answering implicit questions you know we'll have based on your experience.

Okay, Brad, so what gives? The problem occurs when practitioners "educate" folks using doctor-speak - using professional lingo or medical jargon to teach us something that may be way over our heads. When you speak to your patients or clients using your Ph.D, MD, ND (insert whatever advanced degree or credential you have here _____) language, many fail to recognize that the ultimate goal is to convey useful information and to present the material in a way someone can easily understand and later apply and to grow your business. When I was younger, there was a saying it still may be in use, and it goes something like this: "If you can't dazzle them with your brilliance, baffle them with your bullshit." Be brilliant!

Medical professionals should know their audience and speak to us at a level we can understand. I'm not saying to talk down to anyone but to assess their understanding and meet them where they are. If unsure, use everyday language and incorporate technical terms, explaining as necessary. For example, if you are a naturopathic doctor and want to help patients with cholesterol issues, you may be tempted to discuss an important test called Apolipoprotein B-100 (ApoB) Test. The test measures the amount of apolipoprotein B in your blood.

Because ApoB attaches to negative types of cholesterol, causing plaque buildup in blood vessels which can lead to damage and heart disease. Social media video posts often begin like this: "Did you know A-Po-B can test for lipoprotein particles.... "Wow, you completely lost me, and I quickly scrolled past the post you spent an hour working on during the first 5 seconds! Yikes! That's probably not your goal. Instead, I would encourage you to remember whom you are talking to - potential patients who need your care. Instead, I would encourage you to try this approach: "Are you experiencing cholesterol issues or haven't been tested? Maybe you haven't been to a doctor in a while, so I want to tell you about a new test that can make a difference in your life. It's quick, and it's easy. It can change your life. Book your appointment today at: blueearthmedicine.com." See how easy that is; it only takes a couple of minutes to produce a video, and it hits all the points: easy to make, easy to understand, compelling, concise, and it shows you are approachable. Bam! I think you just got a new appointment!

Never assume we (the general public) know as much as you know (you are a doctor - we are not). Now, if your mission is educating other professionals in your field, that's entirely a different story, and to those of you that have chosen this path, feel free to use your doctor-speak and dazzle us with your brilliance!

Now we need to shift our focus to how often you should post on social media. Frequent posting can also improve a brand's visibility and keep it top of mind for consumers, but it's vital to find a balance between frequency and quality. Overposting or posting low-quality content can have a negative impact and turn off folks from following your link, purchasing, or setting up an appointment. I know I've said this before, but this is an excellent time to remind you to download my free marketing plan guide, where you can view suggestions regarding marketing task frequency - it's handy and free. Get it now! Visit: www.bradjohnsonmarketing.com and download it and start using it today. Start Today!

A consistent and strategic approach to posting high-quality content that resonates with the target audience can drive consumer behavior.

Flexing Your Social Media Muscle

In my Marketing Plan Guide, I provide simplified easy-to-follow worksheets that guide you through creating a marketing plan. Unless you're seeking a loan from a financial institution or from investors that require a comprehensive plan, I encourage you to follow my streamlined process incorporating all the essential elements of a marketing plan that address everything you need to consider in your plan but without the headache of creating a banker's version of the plan. The point of **your** plan, whether a business plan, marketing plan, public relations plan, or social media marketing plan, is to provide you with a roadmap to success. Your plans are your compass (or GPS) and point the way ahead, keeping you on track, and without a plan, you'll likely get distracted, lose focus, or get sidetracked. In my Free Marketing Plan guide, I provide an awesome marketing task worksheet that's easy to follow and will help you stay focused and a path forward. In the marketing task sheet, I recommend following a three-part strategy that includes essential, intermediate, and advanced topics; and prioritized by importance and builds over time. That way, you're not jumping too far ahead without first mastering the initial tasks before leaping to more advanced ones.

Constructively building a social media program begins with "Doing with Intention." Always remember your overall strategy and month-to-month, week-to-week, and day-to-day tactics. Don't get caught up in the busy work of posting for posting-sake; that is, only post if you have something worth sharing, which naturally comes from your overall marketing plan and social media strategy. You may create an overarching strategy about natural healing that extends all year, with relevant topics interspersed throughout the year, highlighting the cold and flu season, seasonal allergies, and heart disease.

Know Your Audience, Communicate with Your Audience.

Identifying your target market is one of the most important concerns to consider when building your marketing plan. Likely, you've already heard this from colleagues, professors, mentors, and me (repeatedly), but it's true. Understanding your audience, creating messages that resonate with your people, and being sensitive and responsive to them are key to the success of your business/practice.

Have you taken the time to identify your audience precisely? For many new practitioners, it is tempting to consider everyone in your area your target market; however, that will never be the case. Think of it this way, if you were going to buy a $500 advertisement to spend on a social media ad and only had the $500 to spend, who would you focus your messaging on (and also which platform)? Remember your time is valuable, and you may not factor in the time it takes to create content, design a post, or manage the posting, and while it may feel different than spreading $500, there is a cost associated. It makes much sense to dial in who will focus your energy, time, and financial resources. Let's use an example of a new naturopathic doctor to illustrate a point.

Imagine you are a new doctor interested in women's health and especially interested in helping women work through their fertility concerns. Given this scenario, it makes sense to think of younger women who desire to have a baby as part of your target market. While this doesn't discount other potential patients you may want to see in your practice, this knowledge gives you a direction, something to work with - your target market for this particular part of your practice is going to focus on women of childbearing age, and consequently you'll choose to target those aged between 20-35. Okay, great! This important step will help guide every other decision you make moving forward, from your messaging, content development, marketing materials, and the $500 ad spend you're developing. Current social media demographic information suggests Facebook is by far the most utilized platform on the market, with around 72% of the users being women of reproductive age. Instagram skews toward a younger audience, with 71% aged under 30; similarly, TicTok is increasing in popularity, and as of January 2023, 78% of their users were under 40. Facebook users continue trending older, while other platforms tend to skew younger.

Consequently, given the above assumptions, it may be advantageous for this practitioner to split the ad-buy between Instagram and TicTok. One of the advantages of spending advertising money on Meta (the company that owns Facebook and Instagram) is that you can choose where your ads will be displayed, in case you want to test out the other platform - which is a wise thing to consider. Monitor your ads while they run, take note of any interactions or questions posed, respond promptly, and assess which ads were most effective afterward. Choosing your target market can be difficult but, ultimately, one that'll help you better serve the patients/clients you find most interesting.

Social Media Best Practices

By nature, the social media landscape is in a state of fluctuation, ebbing and flowing with new platforms, updates and improvements to existing platforms, user preference changes, as do the whims of the social media gods.

I'll begin with a list of best practices you can use to enhance your engagement, and later on, I'll share my Top 5 Worst Practices you should avoid. Let's start with how you can become a trusted source of enjoyable, engaging, and valuable content.

Know your Audience - As I've just outlined, ensure you have identified whom you are talking with and craft your messaging to resonate with them. This seems like one of the more difficult challenges for many natural healthcare practitioners because, at first blush, it feels limiting, like "why would I want to focus on a small subset of my community?" By clearly identifying your target audience and understanding their needs, you'll focus more on your marketing collateral, advertisements, ad buys (no need to spend money where it'll be ineffective), and how and where you communicate. It'll make your business development and marketing practices more focused and accessible.

Create Quality Content - Because you know who you are communicating with and created your marketing plan, and have an excellent idea of your target audience, you will craft your messages. Hence, they are relevant, helpful, and visually appealing. Remember, as you're creating engaging content to lean into your brand guide, that way you're consistently reinforcing how your business/practice is perceived. Ultimately your clients or patients want to know how you can help them or, more importantly, how you can transform their lives.

Tag Your Content - It's essential to ensure that not only your current followers can view your content, but you'll also want to ensure that those seeking the type of content you create can easily find it. Hashtags allow you to categorize your content, which in turn, makes your content more easily discoverable.

There are several kinds of hashtags; here are the three most used:

Hashtag (#) - These are labels or keywords used on many social media platforms, such as Facebook, Instagram, and Twitter (e.g., #marketingcoach #health #naturalhealing #naturalmedicine #marektingbook #hashtag).

Mentions (@) - This tag is to acknowledge or notify another user on the platform, often used on Twitter and Instagram (e.g., @bradjohnsonmarketing @blueearthmedicine).

Location tags - These tags specify where the post was created and tended to be used often on Instagram and Facebook (e.g., Seattle, Denver, Rocky Mountain National Park, etc.)

Engage! You may have noticed I keep circling back to the concept of follower engagement. Content that naturally encourages questions, interactions, or comments is vital to building your community and enhancing the likelihood of your post gaining traction.

Engaging with social media followers is essential for building and maintaining a robust online presence for a natural health practice. By responding to comments, questions, and feedback, you can create a sense of community and show your audience that you value their input. In addition, engagement can help establish trust and credibility, increasing brand awareness, client/patient loyalty, and potentially even more referrals.

Here are a few examples of social media posts that a natural medical practice could create:

1. <u>Health Tips</u> - Social media followers love lists, and health tips are the perfect place to play around with this educational idea. Try this: create and share a top 10 list, share natural remedies, offer healthy lifestyle advice, and other wellness-related content that aligns with your practice's philosophy.

2. <u>Behind-the-Scenes Glimpse</u> - Sprinkle these sorts of posts to your social media fans. Give followers a sneak peek into the day-to-day operations of your practice, including photos or videos of you, your staff, the treatment room, and other aspects of the business. I wouldn't post this type of content too often, once per month or less. Unless you can create behind-the-scenes stories that encourage engagement with your followers, it's not worth spending much time on this topic.

3. <u>Patient Success Stories</u> - Readers can relate to the shared stories of others in a way that increases your credibility that you cannot by yourself. In social psychology, we call this concept "social proof" or, more specifically, "user social proof." When we're not sure how to act or behave (or trust), we defer to the experience of others. Success stories written by others can be a powerful form of social proof for your prospective clients. Share testimonials and success stories from patients who have benefitted from the practice's services.

4. <u>Industry News</u> - Followers may also appreciate being updated about what's happening in the profession. By keeping followers informed about the latest developments and advancements in natural medicine and any relevant news and events, you are welcoming them into your world. It feels good

to be included. Sprinkle these sorts of social media posts every once in a while.

5. <u>Community Involvement</u> - By being involved in your community, you become a part of your community, and that's important. How do I get involved? First, join your local Chamber of Commerce to tap into the pulse of your community, attend networking meetings and get to know your business neighbors. People take notice when you showcase your practice's involvement in local events, charity work, and other community initiatives.

6. <u>Be Interactive</u> - The best engagement begins by realizing people go to social media for various reasons, and being a part of a community is high on the list. Followers appreciate posts with a warm, welcoming tone and encourage questions and interaction. Always be cognizant of your messaging and review your posts before submitting - it's easy to get caught up in quickly posting without any solid reason. Post with intention, post for interaction, and post with authenticity.

Ask Your Community - Suppose you want to engage deeply with your followers. In that case, ask them questions and answer them, share an experience, share a favorite photo or video, or share a book that made a lasting impression. I like to share recommended readings with my followers periodically and love to hear back from them.

Pretty Posts - When you take the time to create visually appealing graphics, videos, and photos, your posts will be memorable. You're more likely to get noticed when combined with thoughtful and engaging written content.

Plan Your Postings - Keep tabs on when your followers are most active and plan your posting schedule accordingly. By being active during the times your followers are online, the more likely their eyes will be caught by your posts.

Monitor Success - It's a good idea to stay up to date on how well your social media engagement is working. I'll check the posting insights to see how each post is working, and if I find a winner, I'll review and consider what made it so successful. It's essential to continue to build off your successes and retire posts that never gain traction.

Now that we've covered the best ways you can use social media as a part of your marketing plan, we turn our attention to some of the worst practices so you can learn from my mistakes. These are tips on "What Not To Do."

Top 5 Worst Ways to Use Social Media

All anyone has to do is review social media content to quickly realize the sheer quantity of awful posts clogging up the channels. Social media litter becomes noise, leading to disengagement with the ones we're targeting, turning them off to the essential things they need to hear. In this section, I'll elaborate on the worst social media practices and ways to avoid them.

Jargon - I've mentioned this before, but it's worth repeating jargon builds a wall between you and your prospective clients. I remember when I was in my Ph.D. program learning all about social psychological theoretical frameworks. Most every Friday, fellow students and faculty would blow off some steam at one of the local restaurants/bars, and we'd talk "shop." These talks to an outside observer, or my wife who accompanied me, sounded like this, "blah, blah, blah, theory of reasoned action, blah, blah" - I still apologize and appreciate my wife for enduring the endless, long-winded, boozy and jargon-filled conversations my colleagues and I would share. It's one thing to speak your specialized language with your colleagues. However, when you force-feed potential clients this brand of professional-speak, you're simply closing the door to a possible conversation. I suggest you always consider your audience before beginning any marketing project. If your target market is a lay audience, adjust your language accordingly so they can easily understand what you're saying and, consequently, want to book your services. Be clear and concise and engage with your followers.

Educate with Caution - If you've enjoyed being a teacher, this story will sound very familiar to you. I was fortunate to teach psychology courses at two local colleges when we lived in Iowa. Introduction to Psychology for many institutions is a core course that many students select. As their instructor, I had the front-row vantage point to witness what we can't see when teaching through social media posts or recorded lectures - students' eyes glaze over. They quickly lose interest when we lecture *at* them, and they tune out. When we're teaching via social media posts and videos, we cannot see that look (and once you've seen it, it's hard to get out of your head). Of course, teaching a college course is different from teaching about a topic you know well on social media. Still, many of the same principles apply:

- Make your subject interesting.

- Give solid examples.

- Make the presentation interactive.

- Refrain from talking over your student's head - and if you need to use professional jargon, explain what it means in everyday language.

People often turn to social media for entertainment, connection, and to be inspired to try something new - not to be "lectured at." So keep your messaging simple and entertaining, use everyday words as much as possible, and describe the transformation they will receive when they book an appointment with you. You've got this!

Copy-Paste Mentality - Oscar Wilde once said, "imitation is the sincerest form of flattery." All one needs to do is peruse social media channels to see what he meant. Unfortunately, a lot of "flattery" occurs with the overuse of familiar memes and posting themes. It's gotten to the point where I skip past the nth iteration of another ApoB video posted where a health provider uses jargon and education (yay, a twofer!) to numb me into a fugue state. *(Days later, after such an experience, I wake up deep in a forest in my skivvies, wondering how I got there!).*

Of course, I'm being overly dramatic in pointing out the importance of Doing with Intention - not just copying and pasting. Social Learning Theory helps us understand this form of learning: I watch you, learn from you, and use your style and viola! I've made a post - that looks just like everyone else's. I understand the temptation to lean on other creative folks for inspiration. Still, when folks create a new post simply by copying the template and adding a few new flourishes, we aren't providing much value to our followers - and there are other, more productive ways to get patients, clients, or customers. Instead, I suggest you create only one post weekly if it engages, inspires, and drives traffic to your business, rather than see a flurry of copy-paste-style postings that don't seek to transform anyone.

Memed to Death (or When Cute Isn't Cute Anymore) - The shelf life of cute memes on social media is only a few days. After that, the content, whether in its original form or the reinvented copy-paste version, becomes stale, boring, and no longer cute. Then, why do so many of us squeeze the last bit of juice from this kind of social media fodder? Because it was cute and easy to recycle, and, again, it feels like we're doing something - but that something isn't marketing; it's busy work and accomplishes little towards driving traffic to your business. Remember, we aim to produce valuable and transformative content for our target audience, book appointments, get website visits or email list sign-ups, and sell products or services. How many minutes or hours per day do you spend viewing humorous reels, videos, or stories on your personal social media accounts? If you're like the average person, you spend almost two and a half hours on social media daily - that's a quarter of a workday! Time is precious; make sure you're using your time wisely.

Redundant, Irrelevant & Boring - This is the social media kiss of death, and you do not want to be this person. Here are ten easy ways you can produce <u>terrible</u> social media content:

1. Post low-quality images/videos.
2. Write long and meandering posts that take work to follow.
3. Add 300 hashtags to each post.
4. Produce an excessive number of posts per day.
5. Post only about yourself and not keep your audience in mind.
6. Post videos of you lip-syncing a song or audio file.
7. Post videos of you pointing to text boxes.
8. Post negative, controversial, or politically inspired messages (if you must rant, rant infrequently).
9. Don't proofread your content.
10. Don't engage or interact with folks that comment on your posts.

Parting Thoughts About Social Media

Social media marketing has become essential to any successful marketing strategy. By utilizing the power of social media platforms, companies can connect to their target audience, engage with their customers, and build brand loyalty. However, to make the most out of social media marketing, it is vital to have a clear plan, define your goals and target audience, and regularly track and analyze your results to optimize your efforts.

Moreover, social media marketing is constantly evolving, and staying current with the latest fads and techniques is necessary for staying relevant. As technology advances, new social media platforms and features emerge, providing businesses with more opportunities to connect with their customers. By staying innovative and adaptable, companies can continue to thrive in the ever-changing social media marketing landscape.

Social media integrates well into a holistic marketing program expanding your reach into communities interested in your messages. I support the wise use of social media marketing and leave you with caution: do not over-rely on social media marketing. Social media is a single prong of a multiple-pronged approach to community and brand building, promotions, and advertising. Use with intent and in moderation and avoid the pitfalls I've discussed above.

INTEGRATED DIGITAL MARKETING:

Strategies for Cohesive Campaigns Across Channels

"Digital marketing is not an art of selling a product. It is an art of making people buy the product that you sell." - Hecate Strategy

For a lot of business and practice owners, social media tends to be the go-to platform to "do marketing," and this is probably because so many of us have grown up with social media, use it daily, it's comfortable, familiar, and feels like a safe place. I've mentioned the copy-paste marketing style earlier, and in psychology, there's a term to describe this phenomenon: "social proof." Social proof is where people tend to follow the actions of others to determine what is correct in a given situation. In other words, people are more likely to believe that an idea or product (or social media post) is good if they see that many others have already adopted it. So please repeat after me: social media marketing is only <u>one</u> piece of a marketing program, and I promise to expand my marketing skill set to become super successful!

In this chapter, we get to play around in the fascinating world of digital marketing. Enjoy!

Digital media is an all-encompassing concept and refers to any form of marketing delivered through electronic devices, such as computers, smartphones, and tablets. Digital marketing includes social media, content, email, influence, and video marketing. Topics related to paid advertising, pay-per-click (PPC), and SEO are covered elsewhere in the book.

Digital marketing fits into a marketing plan by complementing and extending traditional marketing efforts to reach target audiences who spend significant time online. A well-crafted digital marketing plan can help a business increase brand awareness, drive traffic and sales, and establish a robust online presence. However, it should be integrated with the overall marketing strategy and aligned with business goals to ensure effectiveness.

Content marketing

"Content marketing is like a first date. If all you do is talk about yourself, there won't be a second one." - David Beebe

One of the tenets of naturopathic medicine comes from the Latin word "docere," meaning "to teach" (i.e., Doctor as Teacher). If you spend time on social media, you'll be impressed by the teaching passions of many NDs. You don't have to be a natural healthcare professional to take notice of all the rich content on social media, Youtube, and other online places. A quick peek will yield teachings of folks making cute, knitted items, jewelry, and sculpture; farmers teaching cultivation techniques; auto mechanics repairing an engine; and those passing along fashion tips.

Each of these folks has one thing in common; they are practicing content marketing.

Creating valuable, engaging, and approachable content is the hallmark of a good marketer, one that sees clients as friends and not simply a dollar sign or a notch on their marketing headboard. I've always considered myself in the relationship business. However, I have yet to meet someone who wants to be "sold anything" in the traditional sense (think pushy car salesperson). Content marketing is the remedy to the intrusive sales approach; instead, it focuses on creating exciting and informative content that is attractive to your target market (have you defined your target audience yet?) — and, ultimately, driving profitable customer behaviors. It differs from traditional marketing in several ways:

1. <u>Focus on the Audience</u> - While traditional marketing is focused on promoting a product or service, content marketing emphasizes providing value to the target audience and building a relationship with them.
2. <u>Education over Promotion</u> - Content marketing aims to educate and inform the target audience rather than directly promoting a product or service.
3. <u>Long-Term Approach</u> - Content marketing is a long-term strategy focusing on building trust and establishing a relationship with the target audience over time rather than making an immediate sale.
4. <u>Multiple Formats</u> - Content marketing can take many forms, including blog posts, videos, social media posts, infographics, e-books, and more, whereas traditional marketing often relies on a single format, such as television or print ads.
5. <u>Measure Success</u> - Content marketing success is measured by audience engagement and behavior (such as page views, social shares, and lead generation) rather than just sales or conversions, which are the primary measures of success in traditional marketing.

"Content Marketing is Relationship Marketing" ~Brad Johnson

One of my favorite aspects of Content Marketing is that this approach is less salesy, more friendly, and welcoming and focuses on building long-term relationships. Holistically, content marketing provides so much valuable content that you can repurpose it for blog posts, newsletter content, or social media posts. Integrated Marketing Communications (IMC) takes this notion to the next level by intentionally creating marketing content for multiple purposes. It's an efficient and practical way to get more mileage from your content and reduce the time you spend on content creation.

Okay, now that we have a basic understanding of how we might utilize our content marketing materials, imagine now you're interested in creating content that describes the value of Vitamin A and wants to share it in various ways.

Here is the essential information: "Vitamin A is an essential nutrient that plays a vital role in maintaining our health. This fat-soluble vitamin is important for vision, skin health, immune function, and cell growth."

Now we can take this primary content and repurpose it for three different uses, blog posts, newsletter content, and social media post:

1. Blog Post:

Title: The Importance of Vitamin A for Your Health

Vitamin A is a vital nutrient that contributes to various aspects of our health. This nutrient is best known for its role in maintaining good vision, but it also has other essential functions. Vitamin A helps keep the skin healthy, supports the immune system, and promotes cell growth.

Foods high in vitamin A include carrots, sweet potatoes, pumpkins, spinach, and cantaloupe. To ensure you get enough of this essential nutrient, consider adding these foods to your diet or taking a vitamin A supplement.

2. Newsletter Article:

Subject: Boost Your Health with Vitamin A

Vitamin A is a must-have nutrient for a healthy body. This fat-soluble vitamin has numerous benefits, including promoting good vision, supporting skin health, strengthening the immune system, and promoting cell growth.

You can find vitamin A in various foods, such as carrots, sweet potatoes, pumpkins, spinach, and cantaloupe. To ensure you get enough of this essential nutrient, consider incorporating these foods into your diet or taking a vitamin A supplement.

3. Social Media Post:

Vitamin A - a nutrient that does wonders for your health!

- Supports vision

- Promotes skin health

- Strengthens immune system

- Boosts cell growth

Get your daily dose of Vitamin A from foods like carrots, sweet potatoes, pumpkins, spinach, and cantaloupe. Or take a supplement! Got questions? Visit our website, link in bio.

#VitaminA #HealthyLiving #vitamins #healthyliving #immunesystem

Designing a Content Marketing Strategy

A content marketing strategy outlines a company's process of creating and sharing messages that resonate with a target audience, ultimately driving profitable customer action.

A template for a content marketing strategy could include the following elements:

1. <u>Objectives</u> -Clearly define the business goals you aim to achieve through your content marketing efforts.
2. <u>Target Audience</u> - Identify and understand your target audience, including their needs, preferences, and pain points.
3. <u>Brand Positioning</u> - Define your brand's unique value proposition and how you differentiate it from your competitors.
4. <u>Content Pillars</u> - Identify the main topics or themes that will form the basis of your content creation.
5. <u>Content Formats</u> - Determine the digital content you want to create, such as vlog/blog posts, live videos, recorded videos, infographics, or static images.
6. <u>Distribution Channels</u> - Identify the channels through which you will distribute your content, such as social media, email, or your website.
7. <u>Key Performance Indicators (KPIs)</u> - Define the metrics you will use to measure the success of your content marketing efforts, such as website traffic or lead generation.
8. <u>Resource Allocation</u> - Outline the resources you will need to implement your content marketing strategy, including budget, personnel, and tools.

For example, a Reiki practice can use content marketing as follows:

1. <u>Identify Target Audience</u> - People interested in alternative medicine and wellness.
2. <u>Develop a Content Strategy</u> - Regularly publish blog posts, infographics, videos, and other educational content that highlights the benefits of Reiki and the services offered by the business.
3. <u>Distribute Content</u> - Share content through social media, email, and other channels to reach the target audience and engage with them.

4. <u>Measure Success</u> - Use analytics to track the performance of the content and adjust the strategy as needed.

The goal of this content marketing strategy would be to establish the natural medicine practice as a trusted source of information and services in its field, ultimately driving more traffic to its website and attracting new patients.

Here is an example of a content marketing strategy for an herbal software company targeting natural medicine practices:

<u>Objectives</u>:

- Generate leads and increase website traffic by 25% in the next 12 months.

- Establish the company as an industry leader in the natural medicine herbal software space.

<u>Target Audience</u> - Naturopathic doctors and herbalists, business owners, and natural medical school program managers.

<u>Brand positioning</u> - A provider of user-friendly, affordable software solutions that help small practices streamline their operations and grow.

<u>Content pillars</u>:

- Product features and benefits

- Industry trends and best practices for natural herbal medicine

- Customer/practice success stories

<u>Content formats</u>:

- Blog posts

- Whitepapers

- Infographics

- Webinars

Distribution channels:

- Company website

- Social media (LinkedIn, Facebook, Instagram)

- Email marketing

KPIs:

- Website Traffic

- Lead generation

- Social media engagement

Resource allocation:

- Dedicated content creation team

- Monthly budget for content creation and distribution

- Marketing automation tool for email and social media management.

Artificial Intelligence and Content Marketing

Early in 2023, Artificial Intelligence (AI) for content creation, design, and programming erupted on the scene, with ChatGPT ushering in a new era boosting the efficiency of programmers, content creators, and students. Therefore, I thought it would be interesting to have the ChatGPT AI create the content for this section and let you be the judge of this early iteration of AI in practical usage. I asked ChatGPT to describe artificial intelligence in the context of content marketing, here's the output:

"Artificial intelligence (AI) is a rapidly growing field that is revolutionizing many industries, including the world of content marketing. AI can be used to improve the efficiency and effectiveness of marketing efforts, making it an attractive option for businesses looking to optimize their strategies.

One way that AI can be used in content marketing is through the creation of personalized content. By analyzing data about individual users, AI algorithms can generate personalized content recommendations and even create custom content based on specific preferences and interests. This allows businesses to better target their marketing efforts and improve the chances of engaging with their audience.

AI can also be used to optimize the distribution of content. By analyzing data about user behavior and engagement, AI algorithms can identify the best times and channels to publish content and target specific audience segments. This can help businesses get their content in front of the right people at the right time, increasing the chances of success.

Another area where AI can be useful in content marketing is in the analysis and optimization of marketing campaigns. AI algorithms can analyze data about user behavior and engagement, providing insights about what content is most effective and which campaigns are driving the most results.

This can help businesses make informed decisions about where to allocate resources and how to improve their marketing efforts.

AI can also be used to automate certain tasks, such as social media management and email marketing. By using AI to schedule and send out messages, businesses can save time and resources, allowing them to focus on other important tasks.

One potential downside of using AI in content marketing is the risk of losing a human touch. While AI algorithms can create personalized content and optimize campaigns, they may lack the creativity and nuance of a human marketer. It is important for businesses to find a balance between using AI to improve efficiency and retaining a human element in their marketing efforts.

Overall, the use of AI in content marketing has the potential to greatly improve the efficiency and effectiveness of marketing efforts. By analyzing data, automating tasks, and creating personalized content, businesses can optimize their marketing strategies and better engage with their audience. However, it is important to carefully consider the potential risks and limitations of using AI, and to find a balance between leveraging its capabilities and maintaining a human touch in marketing efforts."

"Artificial intelligence is a tool, not a threat. It is a tool that can be used to enhance human capabilities, not replace them." - Ginni Rometty

People do not like change; even positive change can elicit a stress response. The same goes for technological advances, with developers and early adopters viewing the changes positively while others expect the worst.

"The development of full artificial intelligence could spell the end of the human race...It would take off on its own, and re-design itself at an ever-increasing rate." - Stephen Hawking

At this point, it's unclear whether the utopian or dystopian view will be the clear winner. But, while that answer unfolds, I sure hope Stephen Hawking is wrong (and if not, I want to thank our new AI overlords for their beneficence). AI is a valuable tool, and I've referred to it often while researching this book and, as in this section, asked for its help.

Now back to marketing. The world of content marketing is in the throes of a significant revolution, largely thanks to the advent of artificial intelligence. If you're not tuned into this yet, it's coming fast and already being used in the marketplace. So I asked ChatGPT with this prompt: "create a social media story for a natural medicine provider describing the benefits of playing outdoors for children." Here is what resulted:

"Nature is the best medicine! Did you know that playing outdoors has numerous benefits for children's physical and mental well-being? Fresh air and sunshine boost vitamin D levels, while physical activity improves strength and coordination. Being in nature also promotes creativity and reduces stress. Let's encourage our little ones to spend more time outside and reap the benefits of Mother Nature's healing powers!

#naturalmedicine #outdoorplay #childhealth #naturopathicmedicine #naturecure #AI #artificialIntelligence #writing #coaching #practicecoach #businesscoach

While AI is still in its relative infancy, all the signs are present that content generation is going to change forever. I suggest testing it out and using it as a tool, not to replace your creativity, but to augment your imagination and as a jumpstart to get writing.

EMAIL MARKETING

"Email marketing is the digital key to unlocking the growth of your business. It's an incredibly powerful tool that allows you to connect with your customers, build relationships, and grow your revenue." - Neil Patel

Email marketing is an essential tool in your marketing toolbox. It has the potential to grow your business in significant ways. Email marketing is integral to your marketing plan, allowing you to reach a large audience and target specific segments. In addition, it is a cost-effective way to reach your people easily.

Before email newsletters emerged, we created newsletters using typewriters and paper - the old-school way! Way back in the day, when I was in the US Navy, each command made quarterly newsletters we'd write and share between each location. By today's standards, those early newsletters were shoddy pieces but were still informative. As one of the writers and editors of those newsletters, we'd solicit content from "writers" within our command, do some basic proofreading, and then print and cut and paste - literally. We'd print and photocopy the article and cut it to size, then put the proof together by sizing it on a letter-sized piece of paper, arrange the stories on the page, secure the cut pieces so they didn't fall off the sheet, then photocopy the finalized page. We'd repeat this process repeatedly until we had an 8-page newsletter. Then, we'd staple it, address it, and mail it out. I remember my first contribution while stationed in Anchorage, Alaska, which makes me chuckle even today. It was titled "Adventures of the Mukluk Gang," I retold the outings my shipmates and I took ice fishing on our days off. I'll never forget stopping early in the morning for breakfast at Iditarod Don's in Big Lake, AK, and gobbling down the best biscuits and gravy of my life!

Incorporating email marketing into your marketing plan is an effective way to enhance the relationship with your subscribers. There are three key benefits of creating an email marketing program:

1. <u>Inexpensive Tool</u> - Email marketing is a cost-effective option allowing you to build deeper relationships, keep in front of your subscribers, and provide meaningful information;

2. <u>Large Audience</u> - You can begin collecting email addresses today and using email marketing you'll be able to communicate directly with folks who already have shown an interest in your services or products. They are already interested!

3. <u>Targeted Messaging</u> - With email marketing, you can refine your list as much as you'd like with the intake form. Once you know whom you're talking to and what they might be interested in learning more about, you can tailor your messaging very specifically.

Creating a robust email marketing program is one of the most important and influential marketing efforts you can spend your valuable time working on. If you already have a successful email marketing program, I'd recommend you peruse this section; however, if you're new to this, I recommend you read through it.

Create an Email Marketing Program

Creating an email marketing program can be broken down into the following steps, first summarized below and then elaborated on in more detail:

1. <u>Define your Target Audience</u> - This is a crucial step in

creating an effective email marketing program. First, you need to understand who your target audience is, what your audience's needs and interests are, and what inspires them to take action.

2. <u>Pick an Email Marketing Platform</u> - There are several email marketing platforms available, such as Mailchimp, Constant Contact, and Aweber. But first, you must choose the best fit for your needs and budget.

3. <u>Build your Email List</u> - You can build your email list by offering something of value, such as a free e-book or a newsletter, in exchange for a potential customer's email address. You can also import your current customer list into the email marketing platform.

4. <u>Create Engaging Content</u> - Your email content should be engaging, relevant, and valuable to your target audience. Ensure to include a clear call to action in each email that encourages your subscribers to act.

5. <u>Design an Attractive Email Template</u> - Your email template must be attractive and easy to navigate. Single-column emails are easier to read than multiple-column templates. Make sure it matches the look and feel of your brand.

6. <u>Test and Optimize your Emails</u> - Before sending them, it's essential to test them to ensure they look good on different devices and email clients. You should also regularly monitor the performance of your emails and make changes to improve their effectiveness.

7. <u>Schedule and Send your Emails</u> - Choose the best day and time to send your emails based on your target audience's behavior and schedule. Ensure you send emails consistently to build trust and establish a relationship with your subscribers.

To maximize the effectiveness of your email marketing program, you should:

- <u>Personalize your Emails</u> - Address your subscribers by name and include their interests and past behavior.

- <u>Segment your Email List</u> - Divide your email list into smaller groups based on common characteristics or behaviors, and send targeted emails to each group.

- <u>Offer Exclusive Deals and Promotions</u> - Provide your subscribers with exclusive discounts and promotions unavailable elsewhere.

- <u>Measure and Analyze your Results</u> - Use metrics such as open rates, click-through rates, and conversion rates to understand your emails' performance and make improvements as needed.

Following this approach and recommendations, you can create an effective email marketing program that engages and converts your target audience. So let's dig into these steps further.

Define your Target Audience

I keep harping on target audiences and plans, and it's for a good reason - you don't want to waste your time and energy doing all this work for nothing. Your time is precious, and it makes no sense to go into marketing work without first nailing down your target audience. Creating a target audience is one of the essential steps in creating an effective email marketing program and your overall marketing plan. First, you need to understand your target audience, their needs, interests, and what motivates them to act.

Choose your Email Marketing Platform.

I cut my email marketing teeth on Constant Contact. Since then, I have used several paid and free email marketing platforms, MailChimp and Send-in-Blue. Frankly, I'm not in love with these services, so I'd encourage you to check out as many as you'd like and review them yourself. The free versions have limitations, including a limited number of free contacts you can add. In addition, those free plans typically include ads. Starting with free plans is just fine. However, as you gain confidence and desire more functionality in your email marketing program, you may wish to consider a paid plan. Choose the one that best fits your needs and budget.

Today, businesses of any size can create attractive, informative, and persuasive communications using free or low-cost email marketing platforms. After you choose an email marketing platform, you'll want to build an email list!

Building an Email List

You can only share your knowledge, tips, deals, and specials with your email list once you create a list. So, let's prioritize this critical task, but first things first: a business must comply with the relevant legal requirements under the CAN-SPAM Act.

The CAN-SPAM Act sets standards for commercial (business) emails, gives email recipients the right to have you stop emailing them, and describes the penalties for violations. For example, a company must obtain explicit consent from an individual before adding them to an email list.

A business must identify itself in all email messages and provide a valid physical address. It also must provide a straightforward way for folks to opt out of future emails (opt-out or unsubscribe button). Furthermore, you must comply with GDPR or CCPA data protection laws for those doing business in the European Union or California.

Building your email list will take time, patience, and persistence, but the long-term benefits will ultimately pay off. Here are some of my favorite ways to build email lists:

<u>Use Opt-in Forms on your Website or Blog</u> - I like to make it super-easy for folks to join my email list, and on my websites, I often include a pop-up email collection app. While you can ask for a complete list of personal information, I'd encourage you to keep it simple and only ask for their email address. Think about how likely you'd be to give specific details. While the extra detailed information would be helpful, it may keep folks from signing up. For my basic opt-in email collection pop-up, I'll design it to be eye-catching using simple/concise language, such as: Join our Newsletter and Get Updates, Tips, and Deals! Over time try out different phrases, and when you find a winner, keep it going!

<u>Offer Incentives</u> - Who doesn't like a freebie? That's right, most of us do, and offering an incentive may be all it takes to prompt someone to join your email list. Collecting an email is a relatively simple process most anyone can accomplish on a website. However, it gets a bit more complex by adding auto-response options; when someone signs up for your offer (and newsletter), they automatically receive the incentive.

An example is Dr. Jill Johnson, ND, of Blue Earth Medicine. She used an incentive to grow her email list considerably. For her offer, she created a Fire Cider recipe. She filmed an accompanying demonstration video to make it easy for her subscribers to follow along and make the recipe.

<u>Host Events or Webinars</u> - This works well for many businesses and natural health practices, especially if you're comfortable in front of people or the camera. Unfortunately, many are not excited about giving talks or planning a webinar. However, if you can push through it, in-person events can be a boon for building your email list. It's also a

great way to create a positive reputation within your community, being seen as a leader, and making it a lot easier for folks to learn about your services and products. So, if you decide to do an in-person event or webinar, make sure to start on time, provide value through quality content, and make sure to leave enough time in the end to answer questions (and create a few questions you can pose for the group to get them comfortable asking too).

<u>Social Media as a Funnel</u> - Social media platforms are designed to be "sticky," meaning they are created to keep you on their page. No wonder cute videos are all the rage; who can leave reel after reel of cute puppy videos? But, of course, those cute videos are interspersed with advertising content - sometimes so subtle that you can't tell they are ads. So, if you choose to accept, your mission is to entice folks to leave the "sticky" social media platforms and head over to your website. So, how do we do that? Persuasive communication is the key to influencing folks.

> **Rant Alert:** Communication is vital. When interacting on social media, we must remember we're building relationships, not solely teaching, instructing, or talking "at" our followers. Communication is a two-way process; when it's just one-way, it feels preachy and lacks connection. Like in real life, people value your knowledge and want to be heard, listened to, communicated to, and acknowledged as intelligent. When a business/practice focuses on "educating" on social media channels, we're missing engagement, and that's what we (those of us tuned in) want. Please talk with us, use language we understand, and try to meet us where we are; that is, communicate using everyday language. If you're a subject matter expert - that's awesome. Still, when you use jargon, you lose the rest of us; I doubt that's your intention. Rant over.

<u>Email Signature</u> - Make sure to add a sign-up link to your email signature. The goal is to make every communication a chance to get folks to sign up for your email list. Including this link in your email signature area is a simple addition and will boost the chance that someone will sign-up.

<u>Happy Customer</u> - If you have customers, clients, or patients that love you, I'd recommend you ask them to sign up (or ask if you can add their names to your email list). Remember you must have their permission to add them to your list and remember you must do all of this email work in compliance with the CAN-SPAM Act.

<u>Selling Stuff</u> - If you're selling products or services, add a sign-up option to your checkout process for e-commerce.

Create Engaging Content

Content is king! I've already discussed creating engaging content and the value of content marketing. Of course, your email content should be engaging, relevant, and valuable to your target audience. Ensure to include a clear call to action in each email that encourages your subscribers to act.

For our businesses, we like to create a messaging plan for the month, refine the topic list, and build out the written content and accompanying visual graphics. Those topics and materials become the email newsletter content and, later, repurposed as blog content, social media posts, and Google updates. In every newsletter, I include links to our appointment page, notes to encourage referrals, and other useful links as appropriate.

I'd encourage you to be cautious with the quantity of content you put in your newsletters. Creating massive email newsletters that turn off many of your readers is easy. However, if you have much information to share, you may consider doing the following:

1. Create a brief story with a backlink to your blog (for the full story).
2. Create a succinct story headline with a clickable link to a PDF.
3. Divide the story for the next issue or two.

My mantra has been to keep your content concise and engaging. Almost equally important as the content of your email newsletter, the design and attractiveness can turn you on or off your readers.

Design an Attractive Email Template

Each email marketing platform offers a variety of templates you can use to share your content with your target audience. About half of your readers will view your content on their smartphone, and the others will use a desktop device. Therefore, your email template should be visually appealing and easy to navigate, with easy-to-read font sizes - remember, not everyone has perfect vision, so shoot for a larger font size to accommodate (I usually default to a 14pt font). Ensure the design features match the look and feel of your brand because consistency is fundamental.

Since you'll be shown several attractive design options, please avoid 2-3 column designs. Yes, they are pretty, but try reading a 2-3 column newsletter on your mobile device, and you'll bounce on to something else. Consequently, I tend to use only 1 column email templates to keep them easily readable. Once I've nailed down the best template for my needs, I recycle the template adding new content for subsequent newsletters. It's okay to play around with your designs as you're figuring it all out, but try to tune it in by the third email.

Test and Optimize your Emails

When I am ready to send a test email to myself, I ensure its accurate and attractive. While I am confident of the quality because it's already undergone several revisions and edits, that's no guarantee it's perfect. Even after all the quality control measures, I use to ensure a final version, there are times when I need to articulate my ideas clearly and miss them entirely. So, review, edit, review, edit, and if you can get an extra set of eyes on it, all the better. Before sending an email blast to my list, I always send a test email to myself and my collaborators. It's a critical practice to ensure you are communicating and that everything is clear with correct information, and that the layout looks right on your devices. Keep a watchful eye out for typos and grammatical errors. There have been several instances where the design and content look perfect on my design screen, and later I noticed mistakes. In those instances, when I view my test email, I may notice the text color needs to be more consistent, font sizes may be off, or an inserted image needs to be clearer. Review the content by looking at the email using your smartphone and a desktop device.

After sending, monitoring your emails' performance and making changes in the next email to improve their effectiveness is essential.

Schedule and Send your Emails

Knowing the best time to schedule your email blasts will optimize your open rates and increase the chances that your messaging is read, links clicked, and appointments established. Therefore, it's essential to determine the best days and times when we improve the odds that your email will be opened and read.

I talk a lot about consistency, timing your email blast, and following a schedule is an important consideration. Email marketing experts tend to send their campaigns during mid-week and favor Thursdays and Wednesdays. The highest open rates tend to occur within the first two hours of a send, with recipients opening most often on Thursday, with

Monday being a close second. Plan your send on a midweek day and schedule the send for hours between 11 am-12 pm or 6-7 pm.

Influencer Marketing

Over the past decade, influencer marketing has exploded on the scene with pretty faces hawking all sorts of goods and services on their perfectly adorned channel with gobs of followers. I understand some businesses successfully worked with social media influencers to sell products and drive traffic; however, my experience hasn't been so rosy.

In case you haven't been paying attention, influence marketing is a marketing a business may use to connect and partner with people with a substantial following who've successfully used their position to influence purchase behaviors. For example, you have an acupuncture business and want to build a relationship with a local influencer focusing on healthy living and natural medicine. In this case, you could offer the influencer a month-long treatment regimen in exchange for weekly positive mentions and encourage their followers to book an appointment. By using this approach, a clinic could leverage the power of the influencer to reach a new customer base who may be interested in the services provided.

Ideally, the influencer will have a solid relationship with their followers. When they promote a product or service, their followers are more likely to trust and believe what's being said and, consequently, more likely to book an appointment.

The hype around influencer marketing is very encouraging; however, my experience in the wine industry wasn't very positive. One would imagine a social media influencer who loves the wine world, and has a large following, would also move the marketing needle a smidge. Unfortunately, this wasn't the case in the several times I attempted to build a relationship with influencers. Instead, it tended to be something like this:

I would often already be aware of the influencer and occasionally reach out to them to begin a conversation. Other times the influencer would reach out to me with their follower statistics, website visitor analytics, and loads of pretty pictures of them holding bottles of wine in gorgeous vineyards. So, I took the bait - too many times, hoping the results would change. During these interactions, I'd invite the influencer to the winery or tasting room, where I'd personally meet them and have a tasting room manager guide us through a complimentary tasting. They'd take photos, ask questions, and we'd provide them a bottle or two so they could shoot some pictures or try the wine later under different conditions. While the influencers were pleasant people, once they began to enact their "influencing," the effect was nil. Too often, the influencer didn't follow through with their promise to post a predetermined number of posts. Instead, they quickly shifted to another winery - for what I can only guess was to fill their wine cellar with free wine.

Even though my experiences have been less than desirable, they may be worth exploring for your business or medical practice. The idea is appealing, but my personal experience left me with a bad taste in my mouth.

Frankly, I'd rather spend my time and energy creating high-quality content and, thus, avoiding influencers by growing my audio and video marketing program.

In my Marketing Plan Guide (available on my website, bradjohnsonmarketing.com), I share a task sheet outlining my recommended approach to holistic marketing. This task sheet helps marketers prioritize marketing tasks from essential/basic, intermediate, to advanced. I encourage my clients and students to follow this progression because I believe that until you've gained solid competency and measurable success using the foundational skills, leaping ahead will only cause your marketing program to become confused. In the next chapter, I discuss using digital images, video and audio to enhance your marketing program.

BRINGING YOUR BRAND TO LIFE:
Maximizing Marketing Impact with Digital Media

With the tools available today, almost anyone with a digital device can take extraordinary photographs, shoot and edit videos, and even create a podcast. There's something special about using your images, videos, and sound in your content creation. Even though stock photos and videos tend to be attractive, they lack the personal touch and seem sterile. Nevertheless, I encourage my students and clients to give them a try.

While living in Alaska, I took up photography back in the 1980's shooting with a Minolta single lens reflex (SLR) 35mm film camera. For the longest time, I shot using the auto feature, where the camera did the heavy lifting, and I simply pointed and shot. The cost of the film made you slow down, compose and think more about the image you were about to snap than when the digital age made the cost to shoot much more affordable. Later, I remember using that old camera during a college photography class, taking photos, processing them in the darkroom, and feeling mighty proud of myself. Unfortunately, my photography skills stagnated during the film days, relying on the trusted "auto" setting and still pointing and shooting.

During the early days of digital advances, I picked up an excellent portable digital single-lens reflex (DSLR) camera that I took into the wilderness as a Ph.D. student doing field research. Still, I relied on the "auto" setting, which produced lovely images. Later on, I upgraded my camera, began an online magazine for the wine industry, and took my photography to the next level by taking it off "auto" into manual settings. A friend reinvigorated my fascination and interest in photography, and my thirst for understanding the complexities of photography took off. Over the coming years, I continued to grow my knowledge and shooting experience leading me to start a small photography business. My photography skills were honed as I developed my marketing consulting business, helping clients grow their businesses aided by my enhanced skills.

While consulting for a small local hospital, I connected with a video production company filming a series of television commercials that introduced me to this new world. I oversaw the production, revised the script, and was on hand during the filming. Later, I took over the script writing for the following commercial and filmed it together. The television commercials were fun, garnered positive attention, and hooked me. Not long afterward, the film company folks and I collaborated on a documentary called Wine Diamonds: Uncorking America's Heartland. As a wine industry insider, I had the knowledge and connections. Over almost two years, we filmed, edited, and finally finished. After that, we began hitting the film festival circuit. The film won a bunch of awards, met a lot of great people, and the film is now available for free on YouTube. Check it out!

Later on, after moving to the Seattle area, I decided to launch a wine industry podcast called The Theory of Wine. Since I had acquired a good deal of knowledge and experience in video and audio production during the filming of the documentary and a series of television commercials and small narrative pieces, I applied that knowledge to this new project where I was to interview winemakers and wine industry folks. It was a blast and quickly grew. Today, I co-host the Blue Earth Medicine Podcast with my wife, Dr. Jill Johnson, ND, where we talk about topics related to natural medicine - you can find it where you listen to your favorite podcasts.

Photography

"High-quality photography can help your business stand out from the competition and attract more customers." - Brian Solis,

This section will briefly cover how you can improve your photography. There's nothing wrong with shooting on auto, but if you want more control over the images you shoot, there's much more to learn using manual shooting settings. Anyone can snap a photo; it's easy, just point and shoot. There's a significant difference between images snapped by an enthusiast and those from a professional. Let's explore how you can improve your photographs with some tips:

1. <u>Learn Your Camera</u> - If you want to shoot memorable photographs, it's in your best interest to learn the functions of your camera, practice like crazy, and experiment with different settings. Open the manual that came with your camera and read it while you have the camera in hand, then explore the various camera settings, shoot some, and then move along. Even after shooting for as long as I have, I still refer to the manual periodically.

2. <u>Composition is Key</u> - For the most part, what you see through the eyepiece of your camera (or the LCD monitor) is what will show up as the image, so if you're shooting a full-length portrait, make sure that you see the subjects feet as well as their head in the monitor. Generally, when we're shooting portraits, we're not wanting to see a third of the image as blue sky unless we're doing something creative. You can improve your composition by observing other photographers' work and emulating their process. Additionally, look into the rule of thirds and leading lines; these concepts can quickly improve your image composition.

3. <u>Exposure Settings</u> - Exposure is the amount of light that hits the sensor inside your camera and is adjusted through three different features: aperture, shutter speed, and ISO. When

you shoot on auto, all of these settings are set automatically by the camera's processor; however, when you take control using manual settings, you'll learn how these three settings can impact your image. When you master these settings, you'll have more control over the images you produce. For me, it rekindled my passion for photography. Give it a try!

4. <u>Use Manual Settings</u> - I've already mentioned this, but you'll learn much more about photography when you take the plunge and use the manual settings. Be brave, open the camera manual, play around in the manual settings, and practice, practice, practice!

5. <u>The Quality of Light</u> - There's nothing like excellent light quality; there's a time of day that's even called the "golden hour" because the quality of light is so good that images pop! Again, I'd encourage you to study the work of professional photographers and, when possible, evaluate the lighting set-up. You can shoot with artificial or natural lighting, and both have a place. Lighting can impact not only the technical settings of ISO, aperture, and shutter speed, lighting impacts the feel of the images.

6. <u>Post-Production Editing</u> - The images straight out of your camera will be fine; however, we want to create memorable images, not just average. I encourage you to find a good post-production editing suite and make your pictures beautiful. I regularly use Adobe Lightroom as my primary photo editor. This package allows me to size the image as I desire (e.g., 1:1 or 1080px x 1080px for an Instagram post) and choose the file type to suit the location you're placing the image (see chapter on Brand for more on file size settings). There are free online editors, but Adobe Lightroom is my go-to and is for many professional photographers.

The thing to remember about photography is that the more often you practice, the better you'll become. Funny how that works, huh? If photography isn't your thing, I'd recommend asking a skilled friend for help or hiring a professional photographer for portraits or business photos. It'll be worth the expense. Now, we turn our attention to moving pictures and video production.

Video Production

"Video marketing is not an option, it's a necessity." - Forbes Magazine

There's something special about a well-crafted video missing from static images or graphics - because they are full of life! Videos are the perfect way to apply the knowledge you've gained in the persuasion and behavior change chapters. By gently using persuasive communications in your video productions, you'll likely move clients and prospective clients to action - to book an appointment, follow your treatment plans, or learn more about what you do.

Turn on most social media channels, and you'll likely find dozens of content creators producing videos - some done well, others disappointingly bad. Earlier in the book, I'd discussed the concept of Doing With Intention, that is to say, creating thought-out content that is planned and well-conceived. Too often, business owners see something cute online, and immediately, without much thought as to whether it fits within the framework of their marketing plan, to follow the Cut and Paste Mentality and produce a video that ultimately has a cringe-worthy quality. This alone is one excellent reason to download the free Marketing Plan guide and plan your marketing. Have you downloaded the guide yet?

The same essential photography tips apply to video production, with a few more intricacies, including audio recording. I encourage you to practice with your DSLR, video camera, or digital device you'll use in your video production work before embarking on your first video shoot.

How to Shoot Memorable Videos

It's important for me to reiterate the importance of following your marketing plan and using the brand guide standards you've created (*you did make a brand guide, right?*) before you start to produce videos. Whether a short and sweet video for social media or a comprehensive and highly polished video for television you should have the right equipment, shooting plan, and know where the video will be posted before pulling out the camera.

Planning your Videos

Before you start producing videos, I need to reiterate the importance of following your marketing plan and using your brand guide standards. Whether a short and sweet video for social media or a comprehensive and highly polished video for television, you should have the right equipment and shooting plan and know where the video will be posted before pulling out the camera.

Prior to starting your video shoot for social media, YouTube, or your website, keep in mind several important factors:

1. <u>What's your Message</u> - What is the purpose of this video, and what do you hope to accomplish by filming it? Make sure you are clear about the ultimate goal of your video. Is the purpose of the video to persuade, educate, inform, or entertain? Remember, attention span is short, so ensure you quickly reach the point. Write down your key message ahead of time so you're clear.

2. <u>Who's your Audience</u> - I keep circling back to the importance of knowing your target audience, so be clear about whom

you're talking to. Clearly identifying your target can shape your message to resonate with those exact people.

3. <u>Platform and Format</u> - Each platform will have different requirements and formats and the audience, so plan accordingly. TicTok and Instagram have shorter time limits than YouTube; additionally, you'll want to be mindful of file sizes if you're planning to host this on your website, as huge files increase the load time of your website.

4. <u>Write a Script and Storyboard</u> - This is where all the planning will pay off. You know your target audience, understand the format and platform, and have a solid messaging strategy, so now you need to write it out in a script. A script or a guide will be handy, particularly for those new to creating high-quality video content. A storyboard is useful for longer-format videos with multiple scenes, locations, and talent. It is a way to visually plan the shots, dialogue, and areas by sketching them beforehand. For most of my short videos, under 5 minutes, I typically only script out the concept. Unless you're exceptionally gifted, there is no need to memorize the script because you can print out a copy and have a friend hold up the paper near the camera so you can read along - it'll save you time and headache. You can also download a free teleprompter app for your digital device, place your script into the program, and read away as you're filming - that's pretty amazing!

5. <u>Location Planning</u> - Knowing where you plan to film is essential when wanting a high-quality video. Pick a location that fits with the message you want to convey and is visually appealing. When thinking about a filming site, consider the location's attractiveness, the ambient sound (we don't want to shoot in a loud, noisy area because it'll make it difficult to hear your voice), and the lighting. Avoid locations that are

busy and loud. There's nothing wrong with shooting in your office, workstation, or home. Mix it up and have fun!

6. <u>On Camera Talent</u> - Chances are you will be the "talent" for the videos you'll be producing, and that's great, but make sure to give yourself space for mistakes. Unless you've been doing this for a long time, you'll make mistakes, and even if you are experienced, you'll probably have a bad day. So, be kind to yourself, give yourself the space to learn, and understand you'll struggle. Still, eventually, your videos will become easier to make, and you'll have fun. Until then, hang in there, take your time, and keep up the excellent work! If you have someone else to serve as your on-camera talent, be considerate and pleasant to them. It's stressful to be on camera and to remember every line and do it flawlessly.

7. <u>Leave your Audience with a Call-to-Action (CTA)</u> - If you follow the above plan, you'll be perfectly positioned to share your message effectively. Ensure your audience knows what to do with the information you just shared before signing off. It's easy to dispense a mountain of facts only to leave the viewer waiting for you to give them something to do. This call-to-action is your chance to move people to action unless you're filming as entertainment. If you've planned your filming well, this should be relatively straightforward. Typical CTAs could be as simple as reminding your viewers to schedule an appointment, like and share your video, try out a new recipe, or visit your website.

Now that you have a video production planning guide, you'll be better positioned to craft engaging, visually attractive videos with a message that resonates and is memorable and prepared for your target audience. Now, we'll focus on what to bring to the shoot.

Video Kit

There are many ways to shoot video these days; however, for this section, I will focus only on digital devices (e.g., iPhone or Android) or digital cameras. One can quickly sink a tremendous amount of money into building a video kit; however, I'm going to advise against it. Instead, I'll outline the essential items you'll want in your video kit and tell you about the nice-to-have things that aren't necessary. This list will help you build your video kit:

1. <u>Get a Great Shot with your Camera</u> - The quality of images captured by your iPhone or Android outperforms expensive DSLR cameras from only a few years back, so it's pretty likely you already have a good camera. A newer DSLR or mirrorless digital camera is an excellent choice to produce amazing videos. Most videos I'm shooting these days are no longer than 90 seconds. The ease of shooting with my Android, quickly editing, and posting is desirable.

2. <u>Be Still with a Tripod</u> - I often shoot solo, so unless I want to shoot a video with my arm extended (blech!), then a tripod is necessary. A tripod keeps your shot steady and eliminates handhold shakiness. Of course, if you have a friend with a steady hand, that's fine, but a tripod with an iPhone/Android accessory to hold it in place is essential. You can find a wide array of tripods, from table-top versions and monopods to carbon fiber tripods. I encourage you to find one that serves the purpose. If you're not shooting professionally, I'd recommend picking up an all-purpose, standard tripod.

3. <u>Audio/Microphone</u> - Many people make videos with terrible sound quality, relying on the microphone inside the camera/phone. Videos using in-camera microphones tend to capture a lot of noise, echoes, and weak audio from the person speaking. Creating excellent audio isn't tricky. As an audio snob, I quickly detect poor audio and find that the worst

videos go hand in hand with bad audio. The easiest way to fix the audio problems is to purchase a lavalier microphone that you can plug into your device. A lav mic is one of those tiny microphones, one that clips on a shirt near the collar. A good microphone will help improve the audio quality of your videos immensely. Check out the online Purple Panda Store for an affordable, lavalier microphone that works with your iPhone or Android. I own a few of them, and for less than **$40**, you'll see an immediate improvement in your videos. Buy one now. (I don't get any kickbacks for sharing this, I want your videos to sound as good as they look).

4. <u>Let there be Lighting</u> - There's nothing wrong with using natural lighting, especially if you're shooting outdoors or have a large window and can shoot inside. However, many people are under the impression that shooting in the sunshine is the way to go. Still, the truth is bright sunshine is hard/harsh light and rarely makes for attractive images or videos (having to squint on camera isn't fun). The best natural lighting happens on overcast or cloudy days as the clouds act like a giant light box, diffusing the sunshine and giving a soft, attractive appearance on film. Suppose you want to shoot outdoors on a bright and sunny day. In that case, I encourage you to shoot from the bright light (out in the sunshine) and position the subject in a shaded area that allows the outdoor light to fill in. Investing in artificial light is a great way to shoot indoors and outdoors when conditions aren't ideal. A wide selection of LED lighting systems or ring lights is easy to use and affordable. Having AC/DC systems allow you to take your lighting outside using battery power and indoors using a power cord.

5. <u>Post-Production Editing Software</u> - A lot of the videos I shoot with my Android are just fine straight out of the

camera; however, periodically, I use the editing software on my device to cut and edit as needed. I know of filmmakers who've shot entire movies using an iPhone. I use my film camera for complex projects and rely on more sophisticated video editing software solutions, such as DaVinci Resolve (the free version is fantastic), Adobe Premiere Pro, iMovie, etc. The editing software has various titles, motion graphics, and tools to make your video stand out.

6. <u>Sweetening your Video</u> - This is for more advanced video creators. Suppose you want to take your videos to the next level. In that case, look at supportive platforms that give you access to royalty-free music, soundbeds, sound effects, transitions, titles, lower third graphics, and motion graphics. Closed captioning your videos makes them more accessible to all users, plus it's just handy to see the words in case someone can't turn the volume up. For clients and some of my personal work projects, I like to amplify the production quality by using fresh motion graphics (those are the graphics that move into a scene, pop, or add movement), titles, quotes (to inform or emphasize), and music. By adding a soundbed to my productions, I find the whole video experience to be richer and more fulfilling. A soundbed is a lower volume, almost unnoticeable track of music playing in the background that adds to the fullness of a video experience. Check out MotionArray, one of my favorite places to get advanced graphics, video clips, transitions, and audio.

7. <u>Don't Run Out of Memory</u> - If you're using your mobile device, make sure you have enough memory to save the videos you're making. It's frustrating to shoot a video, and halfway through find out you're out of memory; for digital camera users, make sure to have a good deal of storage left on your memory card.

There are many places to post your video content; however, before you dive into this choice, please reflect on your target audience and use that knowledge as a guide. In the social media chapter, I discussed various social media platforms. I provided a glimpse at some of the demographics associated with each platform. Think about where "your people" hang out, customize your videos to that particular audience, and place the videos where they'll be seen.

At the time of this writing, Facebook, Instagram, and YouTube are the most prominent players in the world - far ahead of others. TicTok is a rising star where many younger content creators spend their time, but it's not for every demographic. So, remember that just because you're using a particular platform doesn't mean everyone is or, specifically, your target market is engaged. A business owner must balance the time, energy, and resources they use for any marketing effort, so it's impractical to place your video content everywhere. That doesn't make any sense, and it's another example of Doing Without Intention - be clear about your target market and place your videos there. For my businesses, I tend to focus on Facebook, Instagram, and YouTube, embed my YouTube videos on my website, and use those links in my monthly email newsletter. Earlier in the book, I discussed Integrative Marketing Communications (IMC), and repurposing your content is vital to this process.

I want to remind you that my goal is to provide you with the best tips, tools, and tricks to do your marketing; however, it's essential to know your strengths and weaknesses, and if anything I discuss is beyond your ability or desire to learn. You may want to pass for now or hire someone later on. Photography, video, and podcast production are fun and meaningful and help my businesses and clients stand out. So, let's shift our attention to what it takes to create a podcast.

Podcasting

"Podcasting is an incredible medium that allows you to reach and connect with people in ways that no other medium can." - Tim Ferriss

If you're old enough, you may remember "iPods," the small portable square metal device that allows you to download your favorite songs or recorded broadcasts and listen with tiny earbuds. The term podcast was derived from the words "iPod" and "Broadcast" - and, bam, the Podcast was born in 2004.

In 2023 and according to DemandSage.Com, the number of podcast listeners worldwide now exceeds 464 million. Here are some fun facts:

- 5 million podcasts in the world

- 70 million podcast episodes available

- The US has the most podcast listeners in the world

- **"78%** of the US population is aware of podcasts. Out of which, **28%** listen to podcasts weekly."

- 22% of podcast listening happens in the car

Podcasting is a growth market opportunity for the savvy marketer. You should explore podcasts and consider adding one to your marketing plan. Let's take a look at what it takes to pull off a podcast:

<u>Microphone</u> - Quality audio is the name of the game in podcasting, and spending a fortune on equipment is easy. There are lots of ways to become a podcaster, as a solo podcaster or as a team. For me, and the podcasts I've produced, I've preferred to record with a partner. My first podcasting experience happened when I created the Theory of Wine podcast, using an online conference call platform to record audio and video. The camera and built-in microphone were inexpensive

and did a decent job. In addition, I could sweeten the audio during post-production.

To improve the audio quality of a podcast, I encourage my clients and students to consider investing in a good microphone. There are two types of microphones, and I will quickly describe the difference - this is important, so hang in there with me; condenser and dynamic microphones. Without getting too technical, a condenser microphone, such as a recording studio, is a good choice when you have complete control over the recording environment. The Blue Yeti microphone is an excellent and affordable condenser microphone allowing recording in various modes and directions. Depending on your chosen model, you'll have XLR or USB (or both) options to plug into your recording device. The downside of a condenser microphone, like the products from Blue Microphones, is that they pick up all the sound everywhere. That's why having a sound booth or recording studio before using this microphone style is so important. I've used my Blue Yeti to record in my office, only to be disappointed by the fact that I was picking up voices outdoors and car and airplane sounds. It's tough to remove those sounds in post-production.

More recently, I've shifted to an affordable dynamic microphone setup that produces excellent sound quality choosing the U20 Samson microphone. This fantastic microphone came in a kit that included a microphone holder/stand, instruction manual, and both USB and XLR connections and cables (the USB output option is easy to plug into your computer, and the XLR is incredible for those of us with a more technical setup). Now that I've been recording for a while, I prefer the dynamic microphone for its rich sound quality.

<u>Pop Filter</u> - Popping sounds can occur when we're speaking into a microphone, and a pop filter, a little mesh screen that goes over your

microphone or in front of it, helps reduce this problem. This isn't an absolute necessity, but it improves audio quality and is inexpensive.

<u>Microphone Stand</u> - Microphone stands are inexpensive and essential equipment to keep your mic at a fixed distance from your mouth and prevent unwelcome sounds.

<u>Headphones</u> - Having a quality set of headphones is essential. There's no need to spend a fortune; you may already have a nice set in your home office waiting for you to use. Plug your headphones into the headphone jack of your microphone so you can hear your voice. Audio work is more complicated than one might imagine. If you're recording with an external microphone and are on a wireless network, there may be some latency; you may hear your voice in the headset after you speak, which can ruin a sound recording session.

<u>Audio Interface</u> - This is for more advanced XLR microphone users. An audio interface helps convert analog signals into digital signals that can be recorded on a computer. If you're using a USB-powered microphone, this is unnecessary.

<u>Recording Platforms and Devices</u> - Podcasters can use two primary recording platforms to capture audio recordings: computer recording software and portable recording devices. If you have a microphone and a computer, you're almost ready to podcast, and all you need is a way to record and edit the audio. Recording software makes this easy, and with platforms such as Audacity, Garageband (for Apple users), and Adobe Audition, you'll have many options. As an open-source and free digital audio editor and recording application, Audacity is a simple way to get into the podcasting game.

Filmmakers and musicians will likely be familiar with portable recording devices like Tascam or Zoom recorders. For example, my filmmaking partner used a Tascam recorder to capture the audio from our Wine Diamonds: Uncorking America's Heartland filming. When I wanted to improve the quality of my video recording, I purchased the Tascam DR-40, an affordable portable recorder. The Tascam, with its XLR, connections requires using XLR cables to connect with an XLR-supported microphone. The Tascam also has a USB port for external power but lets you connect with a laptop computer. For me, I tend to seek redundancy since I don't want to lose a recording, so I use the Tascam as the primary recording device (it works beautifully and has a micro-memory card) and connect the recorder via USB to my computer (and Audacity) to record in real-time. It's a nice setup for me, and it's working great!

<u>Preparing the Recording Space</u> - Most of us don't have a recording studio to capture sound perfectly, so it's up to us to make our space as recording-friendly as possible. Locate a quiet area in your home or office. Improve the room with soundproofing foam or acoustic panels to reduce the chances of sound bouncing off the hard surfaces and echoing. If you have noisy neighbors, busy streets, or air traffic overhead, try to find a time when it's quiet, the soundproofing I just mentioned will help.

<u>Podcast Hosting Sites</u> - Since I launched my first podcast in 2016, the number of podcast hosting sites and their ease of use has increased. As you review hosting sites, you'll want to remember things such as: 1) how easy the platform is to use, 2) storage, 3) bandwidth, and 4) distribution:

1. <u>Ease of Use</u> - The podcasting hosting site needs to be intuitively easy to use with a minimal learning curve.
2. <u>Storage Size</u> - Many hosting sites allow you to try their platforms before purchasing a plan. The free plans typically allow you up to an hour or two of recording storage space per month. After you post the podcast, it'll stay live for a month

or two before being removed. If you decide to buy the plan, then they'll remain. That's how it was for the Buzzsprout platform I chose to use.

3. <u>Bandwidth</u> - The bandwidth describes how many people can listen to your podcast at a point in time. Larger bandwidths allow for more listeners; however, if you're starting with only a few followers, this won't be a huge issue, but worth keeping in mind.

4. <u>Distribution</u> - I'd encourage you to use a podcasting hosting site that makes distributing your content accessible. That is to say, you'll want your content to be found easily, and the distribution service of your hosting site will allow you to set up and then automatically connect with other channels, such as Apple, Google, Spotify, etc. Ensure to get the embed code from the podcasting hosting platform and embed the code on your website on a page dedicated to your podcast. That way, once you post your new content, it pops up on your website and is distributed to the other podcast services simultaneously.

Here are several podcast hosting platforms: Buzzsprout, Podbean, BluBrry, Fusebox, Anchor, and Sounder.fm, RedCircle, and Captivate. Top picks change all the time, so ask around and review what's available when you're ready to get your podcast going.

Video and podcast production can set your business apart by providing premium content to your community. As a more advanced technique, I recommend that any business wishing to utilize this technology consider the time required to produce quality content regularly. I've seen many websites with blogs that began with good intentions only to languish from lack of attention and upkeep. Suppose you're at a point where video production or a podcast makes sense; spend some extra time contemplating what happens when you get busy. Will your videos or podcast wither? Let me put the time consideration into focus for a moment. Here's a breakdown of how much time it takes to make a 40-minute episode of the Blue Earth Medicine Podcast I produce and co-host:

- Topic creation and Outlining (1+ hour) - As a rule, both Dr. Jill and I brainstorm to come up with general topic ideas. I refine them and create an outline and a series of potential questions that are later reviewed, refined, and finalized.

- Recording Setup and Breakdown (30-40 minutes) - Since we only record monthly, the setup tends to be from scratch each time, including podcast kit setup, testing to ensure it's recording correctly, recording the show, then breakdown.

- Recording (40 minutes) - For the Blue Earth Medicine Podcast I typically plan for a 40 minute show, but that's only a goal, it could be +/- 5 or 10 minutes.

- Post-Production Editing (2-3 hours) - After the show is recorded, it's time to take the recorded content into the editing program to get it ready to distribute. I initially edited the raw audio file during post-production, removing excessive "ums and ahs" and other poor-quality content. After the first round of editing, I'll add the intro and outros. The intro section is a prerecorded piece that describes the podcast's purpose, including any caveats about healthcare information. The outro includes parting words and asks listeners to like, follow, share, and visit our website. Finally, I add a sound bed to the entire interview section to add warmth and richness to the show.

Generally, for every 40-minute show, I spend between 4-6 hours editing and sweetening the audio before posting it to our Buzzsprout channel. In addition to the primary distribution, I take the completed audio file and create a video that's added to our YouTube channel - this takes about another hour or two. With experience, and I have a good deal of that, you can decrease the amount of time spent editing. I value high-quality productions, so it's worth the extra time to create a show that's interesting, fun, and well done.

Parting Thoughts on Digital Media Production

Advanced digital media production is a way to elevate your brand. Over the long term, becoming a consistent content creator of amazing videos and podcasts will position your business to stand out from others doing just the minimum. Of course, not everyone needs to produce their own podcast or video channel; however, if you are interested, you could be a guest on someone's show as an expert in your field - it's a great way to gain some exposure and test the podcasting waters.

There are many ways to enhance your brand presence with digital media, including photography. Producing high-quality images has never been easier, and you can begin today. In addition, advances in video and podcast production make being a producer within reach of almost anyone today, and it's fun and a great way to grow your list of prospective clients, customers, or patients.

HOLISTIC ADVERTISING:
Building Campaigns for Success

"The cost of being wrong is less than the cost of doing nothing." - Seth Godin

The power of advertising is undeniable, and large corporations know the value of creating persuasive advertisements and the importance of keeping market share. Targeting your audience with carefully crafted messages can increase revenue, enhance brand recognition, and improve perception.

Often folks in the marketing, public relations, and communications business refer to two different forms of getting the word out: paid and earned media. Earned media refers to publicity or media coverage that a company reaches through press pitches, social media sharing, word-of-mouth, or other unpaid methods. The goal is to create a buzz about your business, service, or product that occurs without explicitly paying for it. On the other hand, paid media refers to promotions or advertising where a company pays a third party to get the word out. This can include radio/television ads, digital media advertisements, Google Ads, and print media, among other outlets.

If you think advertising is dead, think again. Just look at advertising growth statistics from Statista, during the Super Bowl: In 2003, companies spent $130 million in advertisements, which has increased over time, and in 2022 businesses spent more than $578 million for ad buys!

Of course, a small business cannot compete with multinational companies for Super Bowl ad buys. Still, you can purchase targeted advertising to draw folks to your business in your area, where your customers/patients live. I've done it many times, and it's not as nearly as scary as it may seem. It's likely the most important thing you can do to pull in customers, clients, or patients to your business - and you're probably not even doing this. Yet.

In my professional career, I've had the opportunity to launch several paid advertising campaigns. The most significant challenge to moving forward in this area is knowing how to proceed and whom to contact. To begin with you'll need to speak with an account executive from a media company. This isn't as nerve-wracking as it may seem, but you'll need to prepare for a sales pitch. First, I'll walk you through several personal examples showing you what I went through to get a traditional advertising project successfully launched. I'll discuss digital media advertising later on. An important thing to keep in mind is that it's crucial that you know your target market and ensure the media platform you're considering is the right place to spend your money.

Traditional Advertising

"Traditional advertising methods are still relevant today because they offer a tangible way for brands to connect with their audience. Print, radio, and TV ads create a sense of trust and legitimacy that is hard to replicate with digital ads." - Tim Brown

Traditional advertising refers to advertising channels used for many years, often before the advent of digital marketing. This includes various forms of paid advertising, such as television commercials, radio ads, print ads in newspapers and magazines, billboards, and direct mail.

<u>Newspaper</u> - When I worked for a winery in a larger media market, there were many opportunities to spend advertising money. We had significant resources to allocate toward an ad buy. I'd regularly be hit up by account executives trying to get the company to purchase ads. As a premium winery, our brand was solidly focused on affluent wine

consumers who'd join our wine club and stay with us for years. Joining a wine club is a pricey proposition requiring members to purchase quarterly allotments of as much as a case of wine (12 bottles) per quarter. Like your business or practice, this winery had a particular personality (the brand) that was carefully curated, and the company went to great lengths to protect it. So, we gave it a hard pass when a local edgy urban newspaper approached us - that often ran poorly written articles with off-beat advertisers. Again, it's essential to know your target audience. If I owned a cannabis business, this would have been a perfect advertising option, but not for a premium winery.

<u>Magazine</u> - Magazines have a longer shelf-life than newspapers; likewise, magazine advertisements are more expensive. Most magazines have a specific focus, such as lifestyle, health, travel, food, and spirits. Always refer back to your marketing plan to ensure your target market is captured in their demographic, and if not, you may wish to pass. Once you select a potential magazine, you must interface with an account executive to guide you. If you're not an experienced graphic designer, they'll put you in touch with their design team.

When you first talk with a magazine publisher, you'll want to get a copy of their media kit, advertising specifications (referred to as ad specs), price guide, and editorial calendar. The media sheet will provide you with all the nitty-gritty readership demographics, number of subscribers, and channels they push their product. The media kit sheet is a must-have document. It'll give you the precise information you need to make a well-informed decision about spending your hard-earned money on an ad for this magazine. In addition, you'll need a copy of their price guide and ad specs if you design your ad copy.

Generally, you'll find the price guide and ad specs as a PDF that graphically displays the ad size, layout, and cost. You can often get a discount if you commit to a longer advertising run. First, wait to assess if the ads are worth your spending. Determining if the ad pays off can be complicated unless you can track the conversations. In advertising, conversion refers to a reader's intended action, such as booking an appointment or buying a service or product. One way may be to include a discount code, a unique URL they are linked to for bookings or ask a new patient, client, or customer how they learned about your business.

Magazines produce editorial calendars before the start of each year, which serves as their road map for their publications, highlighting the focus areas and story plans. Knowing about a magazine's editorial calendar is significantly helpful for an advertiser. For example, imagine a local magazine is planning to publish an edition focused on the "Benefits of a Healthy Lifestyle." You've been thinking about advertising, so now might be the time to contact the publisher. But, as always, be forward-thinking and plan, plan, plan!

Most of my experiences working with publishers have been very positive. I've learned a lot from them, especially during my early years (the same goes for working with a quality printer). So, when you find folks that'll help you grow or mentor you, learn as much as possible from them because you'll benefit immensely from those relationships.

<u>Television</u> - When I began my professional career, I quickly connected with media outlets to get the word out, first with newspaper editors and writers and later with local television news directors, assignment editors, and on-air personalities. Reaching out to local news organizations can be daunting for many folks, but if my experience is any indication, connecting with the local media is easy and can yield remarkable results. The public relations section in the book will guide you through the relationship-building process with your media partners and leaning into "earned media" - the free way to get your news, information, and story ideas out to the public.

It's satisfying to see your pitched story idea or news story in the local paper, hear it on the radio, or see it on the noontime news. Those sorts of wins tend to come infrequently but have a real positive impact on your business or organization, a nice ego boost, and it's free. But, of course, television advertisements are not free.

These days television advertising offerings tend to be a mix of traditional and digital media; that is, when you reach out to your television account executive, they'll offer a wide variety of products for you to choose from, and this can be overwhelming to the uninitiated. So, it's a good idea to keep an open mind but also have a good idea of what you're hoping to accomplish with a television advertisement. Frequently your local television station is owned by a media giant and has affiliate TV and radio stations in your area or around the country.

Television advertising is much more expensive than buying newspaper or magazine ads. But don't let that stop you if you are determined; however, I always counsel my clients to ensure this is the most appropriate use of their funds and is targeted enough to warrant the ad-buy.

Several years ago, I was a marketing and communications consultant when a grant opportunity found its way to me, a U.S. Department of Agriculture (USDA) grant. My clients were several wineries and vineyards owners that collaborated and formed a wine trail. This grant offered a no-cash match option (free money) to develop a marketing plan to promote lesser-known agricultural products. With the board of directors' approval, I proposed a course of action, got their buy-in, created a grant application, and ultimately won a $24,000 grant to produce a series of videos about the new cold-hardy grapes of Iowa. The grant funded the video production and the advertising costs to air the 30-second spots in several Iowa media markets. It was a hit! Not everyone has access to free money; grants are available for many industries, and your state or national association should be forwarding those to its members.

<u>Radio</u> - Before I talk about radio, I want to take a quick side trip. Each marketing or advertising approach should align with your overall marketing plan (sound familiar?). Ultimately it is all noise! Now, that doesn't sound good, does it? As marketers, we're competing for the attention of people whom we imagine want our products or services, and in a crowded marketplace, the noise can be deafening, so identifying your audience and making sure your messaging is getting through the noise to the target is a bit of a hit or miss proposition. I'm okay with the "noise" because my voice (your voice) is among a choir of others, and when our messages resonate, we hit the target. That's why I encourage my clients to take a more holistic approach to marketing, testing the waters by trying different techniques. Spend wisely, and always remember whom you're trying to reach.

Like television, radio lets you reach many people in a specific region rather quickly. Knowing your target market will make you better positioned to talk with a radio account executive. Imagine you're a natural healthcare provider focusing on issues related to women's health and midlife, in particular. In this instance, it may make a lot of sense to talk with a radio station whose demographic includes a large proportion of women in your targeted age range (45-55). Once you've identified a station connected with an account executive, you'll work with them to develop a short audio commercial of about 15 seconds. It may go something like this: "Menopause isn't a medical problem or disorder; instead, it is a natural process that some women find difficult. Need help? We're here for you at BlueEarthMedicine.com. Visit BlueEarthMedicine.com to book your free 15-minute menopause consultation today." It's essential to be specific, concise, clear, and put into a rotation the messages your target will most likely hear. The account executives will propose several time slots, some during peak drive time and others during off time. They will sometimes give you free slots when spots open up in their schedule.

It's worth repeating: tracking the success of your ads is very important! There isn't any sense in paying for an ad if you don't know if it's working for you.

I have a home recording studio, so I've recorded the audio spots (radio ads) I've used for radio ads and incorporated the content for static or motion ads in my social media work. There's nothing like using the voice of the doctor, practice, or business owner to be the "voice" of the business. Of course, this isn't essential, but it's a nice touch if you're comfortable with this sort of public speaking.

<u>Billboards</u> - Mass communication is like casting a big net into the water. You'll never know what you'll catch, but there is still some appeal to using billboards as part of a more significant, broader outreach effort. Billboards are a pricey alternative to reaching a sizable undifferentiated audience, especially if the board is along a busy stretch of freeway. Several years ago, when working for a winery employer, we came across some free grant money (yay, free grant money!) that allowed us to purchase ad space from a billboard agency. With the winery about 6 miles north of a busy transcontinental highway, many eyes saw our billboard. Behind the tasting room bar, where our attendants positioned themselves while serving and interacting with our guests, we'd have them ask, "how did you learn about us?" I always encourage, plead and beg my clients to ask this question from every new customer, client, or patient because it's an easy way to gather this critical marketing data. I created a handy tally sheet, hidden under the counter of the tasting room, where employees could refer to, check a box with a simple hash mark, and every week I'd compile the data.

You can do the same thing by creating your sheet and including the following checkboxes: recommended by a friend, seen on social media, billboard, tv spot, radio ad, etc. It's super helpful information and will help you dial in your paid/earned marketing efforts. For example, after spending the next couple of months collecting data, you may notice most of your new clients found you through Google Ads. As a result, you may want to pull back on other ad spends and reallocate or hold off and continue to track and evaluate. Chances are you'll find one or two channels that will be the best option for your business.

What did we learn? The boards are visually appealing, and loads of travelers take notice. Still, ultimately, the sign wasn't all that helpful in drawing in winery customers. Upon reflection, we should have realized that this shotgun approach to marketing wouldn't be all that productive in driving traffic to our winery. Nevertheless, it was an important (and inexpensive) exercise that suggested we could spend our advertising dollars more wisely in more productive ways.

<u>Direct Mail</u> - Direct mail advertising may seem like old-school marketing, and in many ways, it is; however, it's also a relatively easy way to quickly reach a very targeted large audience with a single pitch. I'm not going to go into great detail with this method, but instead provide you with a few tips to get the ball rolling:

> <u>Bulk Mailing</u> - Any business interested in using bulk mailing should connect with the United States Postal Service (USPS) and review how you can work with a commercial company or do it yourself. You can purchase a mailing list from many companies that contain addresses from the zip code you are interested in sending your mail to (also includes vital demographic information) that you can use to print your labels to mail off and do it yourself. (Source: https://faq.usps.com/s/article/How-do-I-get-Started-with-Bulk-Mailing)

<u>EDDM</u> - TThe USPS also has a more streamlined program called Every Day Direct Mail. According to the USPS, "Use Every Door Direct Mail® (EDDM®) services to promote your small business in your local community. If you're having a sale, opening a new location, or offering coupons, EDDM can help you send postcards, menus, and flyers to the right customers. Use the EDDM Online Tool to map ZIP Code(s)™ and neighborhoods—even filter by age, income, or household size1[1] using U.S. Census data." (Source: https://www.usps.com/business/ every-door-direct-mail.htm)

It's been a while since I've used direct mail marketing. As an executive director of a nonprofit, I would utilize the USPS Bulk mailing service to save time and money for my direct mail efforts. Each quarter we'd send progress reports and updates to several thousand people. Over the years, we had amassed an extensive mailing list that we'd sort by zip code and affix the labels on the cards; then, bring those cards, which were banded together by zip code, and take them to the Bulk Mail office at our local post office. As a result, we saved a good deal of money by avoiding the first-class postage fee.

I was collaborating with another consultant working with a local hospital for a while. During those days, we created, wrote, and produced several large postcard-size flyers and magazines that we wanted to send to every home within a specific geographic region. Again, Every Day Direct Mail (EDDM) was the clear winner saving us time and money getting these pieces out to our community.

It's been a long while since I've relied on the USPS to deliver my printed marketing materials. Still, upon reflection, I'd say the

---

1. https://www.usps.com/business/ every-door-direct-mail.htm#a5c02393e59c943d6a75a9241140faca31

experience of working with them and the outcomes were generally positive.

Digital Advertising

"Digital advertising is a powerful tool that allows businesses to connect with their customers and reach new audiences in a way that was not possible before." - Gary Vaynerchuk

In many cases, the more extensive traditional media companies that once dominated the print and broadcast media landscape have also successfully transitioned into digital media. Just look at The New York Times, which is still the dominant print newsletter with a potent online presence, along with associated radio programs and affiliated with other news agencies. The NYT is more powerful than ever today. In addition, with the growth of digital paid media, Pay-Per-Click (PPC) advertising emerged as an outgrowth from traditional advertising.

Pay-Per-Click (PPC) Advertising - PPC is a digital marketing method in which an advertiser pays each time a user clicks on one of their ads. In PPC advertising, ads are displayed on search engines like Google, social media platforms like Facebook, or websites that partner with advertisers.

A natural health business can benefit from using PPC advertising in several ways:

1. Targeted Reach - PPC advertising enables organizations to target specific groups of people based on factors like demographics, interests, and behaviors.
2. Cost-Effective - PPC advertising operates on a bidding system, allowing organizations to set a budget and only pay when users click on their ad.

3. <u>Measurable Results</u> - PPC advertising provides detailed data and metrics on ad performance, allowing organizations to measure their campaign success and modify their strategy accordingly.
4. <u>Quick Results</u> - PPC advertising can produce results quickly, unlike other forms of digital marketing that may take longer to deliver results.
5. <u>Increased Visibility</u> - PPC advertising increases an organization's visibility and exposure, which can lead to increased brand recognition and more potential customers.

While prominent traditional media players are still in the game, the digital giants and social media powerhouses have taken a significant market share of the advertising sphere. Over the past two decades, advertising dollars have shifted from traditional to digital channels such as social media, search engines, and mobile apps. As a result, the most prominent digital advertising players today are Google and Facebook.

<u>Google</u> - Undoubtedly, Google is the most significant player in the digital advertising game, with tentacles extending to almost every nook and cranny of the Internet. But how big of a deal is Google to search? At the time of this writing, Google is the number 1 search engine in the world, racking up about 84% of all searches; the next closest is Bing which averages around 9%.

Out of all the paid advertising options we've tried over the years, Google Ads is the best way for our targeted messages to reach our intended audience. While this section is about paid advertising, it's important to understand that having a finely tuned website and updated Google Business Profile (formerly called Google My Business) will enhance search outcomes for prospective clients. So let's take a brief look.

Google Business Profile is a free tool allowing companies to manage their online presence on Google. For example, companies can create a listing on Google My Business that displays their name, address, phone number, business hours, and other relevant information. This listing appears in Google's search results and on Google Maps when users search for a business similar to theirs.

Because Google is ubiquitous in search, it is paramount that your business gets noticed by Google, and the first step is ensuring your website is easily found and optimized for search; likewise, if you haven't yet, secure your Google Business Profile and regularly update with fresh content and make sure your business hours are kept current. Now, let's turn our attention to paid advertising opportunities on Google.

Google Ads, formerly known as Google AdWords, is an advertising platform that allows businesses to create and display ads on Google's search engine results pages and other websites in the Google Network. Advertisers bid on specific keywords related to their company or product. Their ads are then displayed to users who search for those keywords or visit websites that are relevant to those keywords. Setting up a Google Ads account and launching your first Google Ad Campaign is a relatively streamlined process that begins with setting up an account.

Setting up Google Ads for a new business can be an effective way to gain visibility and drive traffic to your website quickly. While the below list of general steps was accurate in 2023, there is a good likelihood that changes will occur that'll streamline and simplify the process by the time you read this content; however, here are the general steps to follow:

1. <u>Create a Google Ads Account</u> - If you don't already have one, create one by visiting ads.google.com and signing up for an account.

2. <u>Set up Billing</u> - You'll need to set up your billing information before running ads. Set up by clicking on the gear icon in the top right corner of your account and selecting "Billing & payments."

3. <u>Define your Campaign Objectives</u> - Determine what you want to achieve with your ads. Do you want to boost web traffic, induce leads, or propel sales? Having a clear objective will help you create more effective campaigns.

4. <u>Identify your Target Audience</u> - Determine who your ideal customer is and define their characteristics, such as age, location, interests, and other demographic information.

5. <u>Select Keywords</u> - Research and select the keywords your target audience is most likely to search for when looking for your products or services.

6. <u>Create your Ad Campaigns</u> - Using your campaign objectives, target audience, and selected keywords, create your ad campaigns. This will include setting your budget, building your ad copy, and selecting your ad format (text, image, or video).

7. <u>Launch your Campaigns</u> - Once you've created a campaign, launch it, monitor its performance, and modify as needed to optimize your results.

8. <u>Monitor and Optimize</u> - Continually review your campaign performance and make changes to enhance its effectiveness. This could include adjusting your targeting, keywords, ad copy, or budget.

Here are several tips to keep in mind when setting up a Google Ad campaign:

1. <u>Search Your Competition</u> - Before you begin, do several Google searches for businesses like yours. For example, if you are a chiropractor, you may wish to search for "Chiropractors

Near Me" and see which companies appear. Review their ad copy, notice where they show up in the list, and you can begin to think about the ad copy as your review, but make sure the copy you write is fine-tuned for your business.

2. <u>Set a Modest Budget</u> - It's a good idea to start with a small budget and gradually increase it as you learn and optimize your campaigns. When creating your ad sets, Google will display the range of budgets competitors currently use. We've used this range as a starting point, and it's been a valuable way to set an initial budget. After a few weeks, you can determine whether you're in the ballpark or need to increase your budget.

3. <u>Make Use of Negative Keywords</u> - Use negative keywords to exclude irrelevant searches. You'll create a keyword list, but over time Google will add to this list which can cost you if you're not paying attention. For example, for my wife's naturopathic medicine practice, I established a relevant list of keywords, such as "Naturopathic Doctor, Naturopathic Medicine, Natural Medicine, Integrative Medicine, Naturopathic Doctor Near Me," and over time, I've had to cull terms such as "Bob's Pizza, Massage Therapist, 1111 Nature Way Rd.," - Review weekly and when inappropriate keywords appear, add them to the Negative Keyword List.

4. <u>Test, Test, Test</u> - Test different ad copy and target audiences to see what works best for your enterprise. You can create four other ads for each ad campaign, allowing you to hone the titles and content. Make sure to display your profession prominently. For example, if you own a massage business, you could add these three titles: Massage | Sports Massage in Grand Rapids| Deep Tissue Massage

5. <u>Try the Keyword Planner</u> - Use Google Ads Keyword Planner to research and choose the most effective keywords

for your campaigns. https://ads.google.com/home/tools/ keyword-planner/

6. <u>Review Your Quality Score</u> - Keep an eye on your Quality Score, as it can impact the success of your campaigns.

Setting up Google Ads for a new business can be a complex process. Still, by following these steps and continuously monitoring and optimizing your campaigns, you can create compelling ads that drive traffic and sales to your website.

As a small business owner/practice owner, you probably don't have unlimited financial resources, so you'll have to decide how and where to spend your advertising dollars. Where will you get the biggest bang for your buck? In other words, if you have a fixed budget of, say, **$350 per month**, where will you spend it? As I have outlined above, there are many ways to spend your money, and countless experts eager to take your money. Still, it would be best if you were confident of your choice. Of the paid advertising options available to me, I have found Google Ads to be the best spend for the money - in terms of suitable metrics to evaluate the efficacy of the ad, ability to narrowly target, keyword targeted, and getting prospective clients to set up an appointment. The better your ad, the better your chances of connecting with your target audience. I encourage all my students/clients to ask, "how did you find my business?" - I call this ground truthing. Ground truthing is a term used in mapping that uses both overhead imagery combined with on-the-ground observation to ensure that what we believe we see is real. So, for this example, my Google Ads metrics suggest ten people called or visited my website aligns with my question to 9 new patients after asking them how they found me.

In summary, Google Ads is an advertising platform that businesses use to promote their products and services. At the same time, Google Business Profile (formerly known as Google My Business) is a tool that companies use to manage their online presence and make it easier for customers to find them.

The world of online advertising isn't limited solely to Google. In today's market, the two prominent players are Google and Facebook; we'll now turn our attention to Facebook.

<u>Facebook</u> - According to the popular social media management software platform, Hootsuite, "one out of every five digital ad dollars is spent on Facebook. In addition, the platform's roughly 2 billion monthly users spend an average of 53 minutes a day on the site - more than Snapchat (33 minutes) and Instagram (32 minutes)."

As an early adopter of social media and of Facebook, I've seen how this platform has morphed over the years into a significant player in digital advertising - at the expense of a quality user experience. Meta, the parent company of Facebook, Instagram, WhatsApp, Messenger, and other lesser platforms, makes setting up a business page and creating a business advertising account easy.

Despite our familiarity with these platforms, it's becoming increasingly clear that spending advertising money with the Meta platforms isn't paying off. Yet, I periodically spend a few bucks on seeing if anything has changed. When I first began advertising with Facebook years ago, the algorithm gave my paid posts a decent reach and excellent engagement; however, that has changed in the past several years. As a result, my paid advertisements barely get noticed, and any advertisements that did get some attention rarely lead to a single conversion.

> **Let's talk about Conversions** - In marketing, conversion refers to a desired action taken by a user on a website or digital platform. A conversion may include a variety of activities, such as buying a product or service, completing

a form, showing intention to make an appointment, subscribing to an email newsletter, or downloading an app.

A marketing conversion occurs when a user completes one of these desired actions, indicating that they have moved further down the marketing funnel and are more likely to become a customer or engage with a brand meaningfully.

The conversion rate is the proportion of website visitors who complete the desired action out of the total number of users who visit the website or landing page. Marketers use conversion rates as a key performance indicator (KPI) to measure the effectiveness of their marketing campaigns and optimize their efforts to improve conversions.

Unless you've trained as a marketing, communications, or public relations professional, all of this may seem overwhelming or unnecessary. However, my coaching philosophy is grounded in what I believe to be one of the essential parts of being a business owner: an owner must know how every facet of their business works. I'm sure you didn't go to medical school (or whatever program or path you've taken) to be a marketer or an entrepreneur. Still, here you are, starting or striving to build a successful business, and part of that means you need to know how it works from the ground up, how to grow it, and how to spend wisely.

Spending Wisely & Measuring Effectiveness

After spending a lot of your start-up capital on rent and utilities, equipment, office supplies, and a website, a new solo practitioner or small business owner may be overwhelmed by the need to spend more money on advertising. That's why it's so important to choose a platform that makes the most sense for your business and ensure your advertising is paying off. That's where holistic marketing comes into focus - you see, holistic marketing isn't a single approach to reaching an audience. Instead, it's an integrative approach that values advertising, public relations, digital marketing, email marketing, content marketing, social media marketing, and good old-fashioned in-person, hand-shaking networking. The value of Holistic Marketing comes from the idea of creating high-value content shared across various platforms and for numerous purposes. As a result, it saves time and money and makes sense from an operational standpoint.

Planning is the key to many of your marketing goals and is essential to your success. The same is true for any paid advertisement program you decide to establish. Paid Ad plans generally include these key features:

- Defining the advertising objectives

- Identifying the target audience

- Selecting the advertising platforms

- Determining the budget

- Creating ad content

- Setting the advertising schedule

- Measuring the advertising performance

Let's delve into how to measure the effectiveness of your paid advertisements.

We discussed this briefly earlier in the book, but here we offer a more thorough examination. There are many ways that you, an advertiser, can measure the effectiveness of a campaign; these include:

1. <u>Sales and Revenue</u> - One of the most direct ways to measure an advertisement's effectiveness is to track the increase in sales

and revenue. By monitoring the changes in sales before and after the campaign, an advertiser can assess the impact of the advertisement on the business.

2. <u>Brand Awareness</u> - An advertiser can also measure an advertisement's effectiveness by monitoring brand awareness. Effectiveness is measured using surveys, polls, or focus groups to determine if the ad has increased brand recognition and recall among the target audience.

3. <u>Website Traffic and Engagement</u> - Another way to measure an advertisement's effectiveness is to track website traffic and engagement. By monitoring the number of website visitors, the bounce rate, and the time spent on the website, an advertiser can determine if the advertisement is driving traffic to the website and if visitors are engaging with the content.

4. <u>Social Media Metrics</u> - Advertisers can also measure the effectiveness of an advertisement by monitoring social media metrics, such as likes, shares, comments, and followers. This can help determine if the ad resonates with the target audience and drives engagement on social media platforms.

5. <u>Cost per Acquisition (CPA)</u> - Advertisers can track the cost per acquisition, which is the cost of acquiring a customer, to determine an advertisement's effectiveness. This metric can help assess the advertisement's return on investment (ROI) and determine if it is generating revenue at a cost-effective rate.

6. <u>Ad Engagement and Conversion Rates</u> - Advertisers can also track the ad engagement and conversion rates to measure an advertisement's effectiveness. A business can track how many people are clicking on the ad and taking action, such as filling out a form or making a purchase.

The digital revolution has allowed businesses to grow and thrive like no other time in history; however, one of the downsides of our reliance on digital media is that we've lost connection with face-to-face interactions and an entire way to building business, one person at a time.

Other Strategies to Grow Your Business

Even as the Internet was first coming to life, Futurists envisioned a time in the not-too-distant future (today) when somebody would deliver groceries and products to your home, in-person relationships would diminish, and people would, in their terms, turn inward and cocoon. That is, we'd begin to live in self-imposed isolation with minimal social contact. The recent pandemic did us no favors in reversing the isolation we feel, leading many of us to feel lonely, depressed, anxious and wishing to avoid groups of people. It makes sense if we are hoping to keep ourselves safe and germ-free; however, the negative social consequences of self-imposed isolation when trying to build a business can get in our way.

Over the next couple of pages, I'll describe time-tested ways individuals and businesses have used to others, spread the word about their business, and do the unthinkable - shake hands with new people. Of course, I jest, sort of. Many of us have developed social phobias and anxiety about gathering in public. I count myself as one of those folks, but if we can get past our fear, shyness, or insecurity, there is a good chance you'll open the door to those who need your products and services.

There is nothing like being in person, having a real-life conversation, networking, and hosting a talk to convert the "maybe interested" into a "client." The list below illustrates the variety of ways you can grow your brand to get the word out:

<u>Join the Chamber of Commerce</u> - Regularly attend meetings, share updates with them, and network. Chamber members are typically business members who live in your community, are a great source of referrals, and can be lucrative prospects.

<u>Give a Talk</u> - Many organizations are looking for speakers every month. You can create a presentation and offer a talk in a community space or seek other opportunities in your area.

1. <u>Library</u> - set up a talk at the library
2. <u>Service Clubs</u> - connect with one of your service clubs and learn what it takes to offer a talk. A service club is an organization serving a community or local cause.
3. <u>Reading Groups</u> - reach out to the local book club to see if they allow folks to give talks.
4. <u>Guest Lecturer</u> - identify a local college or university and offer to provide a talk about an exciting topic. Reach out to relevant colleges, departments, or programs that fit your industry well.
5. <u>Conference Speaker</u> - sign-up with your state or national association to present on a topic of interest.

<u>Engage in your Community</u> - if you have a business or medical practice, you are already in the community; now it's time to fully engage with your community by being more involved.

1. <u>Volunteer</u> - giving back to your community through service will demonstrate your commitment to the community, allow you to meet new people, and give you access to other professionals who may value your work.
2. <u>Board of Directors</u> - there are many opportunities to give back as a board member. Seek out opportunities to be active on a board. Your state or national professional organization

always seeks member support; your local nonprofit organizations are endlessly looking for engaged folks to help. In addition to giving back, you'll meet folks with a common interest and extend your reach by getting to know people not necessarily in your field.

3. <u>Give Pro Bono Services</u> - dedicate a certain amount of your workload to giving free services to people in your community.

<u>Join a Service Club</u> - a service club is a community organization with a specific focus. Here are several service clubs to consider:

1. Rotary Club
2. Lions Club
3. Kiwanis Club
4. Optimists Club
5. Toastmasters International

<u>Network</u> - Networking aims to grow the number and quality of contacts within your community. Being connected is a crucial part of growing your business and practice.

1. Attend Chamber of Commerce events.
2. Attend community-organized events.
3. Be involved with state association events.
4. Attend conferences and workshops.

<u>Join or Create a Networking Group</u> - If your area doesn't have a networking group for an interest area you have, consider creating one yourself.

1. Start/Join a Mastermind Group.
2. Start/Join a business networking group.
3. Start/Join a marketing networking group.

4. Start/Join a natural medicine networking group.

<u>Join an Organization</u> - You can join an organization for personal or professional development.

1. Join your state association.
2. Join your national association.
3. Be active in the meetings and gatherings of the organizations you've joined.
4. Volunteer for your organization.

Being involved in your professional organizations and your local community and engaging in interest area communities will benefit your business and personal life. Engaged community members value other members who are involved, resulting in more connections, increased visibility, clients, and more profound life satisfaction at a personal level.

INTEGRATED PUBLIC RELATIONS:

Aligning PR Strategy with Overall Business Goals

"Public relations are a key element in the success of any business venture. They can make the difference between success and failure." - Richard Branson

I have a soft spot in my heart for public relations and the relationships I've developed with people in the media. After leaving the US Navy in the late 1980s, I entered an undergraduate program at Central Michigan University studying Parks and Recreation Administration. You may wonder how in the world did your parks' training equip you to work with the media and build a marketing empire (okay, no empire, but at least a serfdom)? The training included understanding finance and budgeting, fundraising, marketing, public relations, and managing a multi-million dollar public enterprise. Much of the coursework required us, the students, to create and launch a recreation offering for our community and to pull it off.

For a student assignment, my student colleagues and I decided to work on a volksmarch at one of our rural county parks. According to Wikipedia, a *"Volksmarsch"* is a German word for "people's *march"* and a form of non-competitive fitness walk developed in Europe in the mid-late 1960s. We aimed to encourage outdoor recreation and for visitors to explore several miles of beautiful nature trails in one of the parks. Our efforts required me to contact the media to get the word out. The results were encouraging, we had news stories published in the local newspapers before the event, and reporters were on hand on the morning of the event - it was a hit, and I was hooked!

I sometimes use public relations and paid media at the same time; however, public relations (PR) and earned media are just related concepts that refer to different aspects of a brand's communication strategy.

In my experience, public relations focuses on managing the communication between an organization and its stakeholders, such as target customers, employees, investors, and the media. PR aims to create a positive image of the organization and build relationships with the target audience. PR may involve various activities, such as media relations, crisis management, event planning, and social media management.

There's something special about seeing a social media post go viral or having a pitched story picked up by the local media. Earned media, compared to PR, refers to the publicity an organization receives through media coverage, social media sharing, or other forms of user-generated content. Earned media is also often seen as more credible than other forms of advertising because it is based on an independent, third-party endorsement. Examples of earned media include news articles, blog posts, social media shares, and online reviews.

While PR may involve efforts to generate earned media, such as pitching stories to journalists or cultivating relationships with bloggers and social media influencers, it also includes other activities, such as internal communication, branding, and community outreach. Earned media, on the other hand, is a specific type of media exposure that is acquired through the quality of an organization's products, services, or messaging.

What is Public Relations and Why is it important?

For most of my professional career, I practiced public relations using an intuitive approach, seeing PR as a relationship-building process, following my gut, and rarely without much of a plan. Using this less structured approach worked well for a long time when I had a good working relationship with my local media market; however, things changed once I moved across the country to a new media landscape. I no longer had contacts within the media market, didn't have relationships with reporters or news assignment editors, and I was left frustrated and feeling inept. Building these relationships takes time, persistence, and commitment, so it's essential to plan accordingly. And while early in my career, I neglected to have a formal PR plan, later, I've found this to be incredibly useful and has fine-tuned my efforts and brought greater focus to my planning and, ultimately, more success.

Before moving to the Seattle area in 2016, I was a PR rockstar, and in a month or two, I knew nothing or nobody. Yikes, it was time to rebuild my list and my relationships. So when I landed a marketing and communications manager position with a premium winery, and my workload increased to the point of losing my mind, the owners brought on a public relations consultant - a publicist. In my professional life, I'd never worked with a publicist before; however, I have worked in that capacity for many of my past clients, but I never worked directly with one. It revealed how an intelligent and connected publicist could make inroads it'd take years for me to build.

There is nothing like working with a professional publicist who has solid media credentials and connections in the markets you're interested in reaching. From the start, we built a public relations plan creating quarterly goals and anticipated topics we'd focus on and pitch. We'd frequently make planned pitches (e.g., new wine released, recent wine awards, new philanthropic things we did, etc.) and had much success. Understanding the "mood" of the media is another important thing a good publicist will keep in mind because, as we saw during the early years of the Covid-19 pandemic, the news agencies were keen on "soft, positive news stories" and as a winery, we had lots of good news to share. However, as society began to handle the disease better, the news business shifted from feel-good stories to "hard news stories," leaving our feel-good stories discarded. The news organizations were not interested in our gold medal-awarded wines, were less interested in hearing about our philanthropic projects and donations, and didn't care much about rich folks who owned yet another winery or vineyard. It was a tough transition.

Planning is vital to any successful business. In this book, I've outlined many planning processes that may feel overwhelming to a new business owner. Indeed, you can only do so many things at once, so you'll need to prioritize projects. I advise you to begin with the essential business and practice tasks, then build your marketing plan. The marketing plan will guide building a following, connecting with your target audience, and growing your business. While nice to have, a public relations program isn't necessary from the outset. Although there is still much value to creating a PR program, a potent PR program can be helpful for:

1. <u>Managing Reputation</u> - By proactively managing your business's image and communicating effectively with your target audience and key stakeholders, a PR program can help to build and maintain a positive reputation for your business and practice.
2. <u>Enhancing Brand Awareness</u> - A PR program can help boost awareness of your business, products, services, or brand, which can translate into increased sales and profits.
3. <u>Boosting Credibility</u> - By providing valuable, accurate and transparent information to the public, a PR program can help to build credibility and trust in your business/practice.
4. <u>Influence Public Opinion</u> - A PR program can help to shape

public perceptions and attitudes towards your practice, products or services.

5. <u>Crisis Management</u> - A well-honed PR program can help a business to effectively communicate and manage its response to crises, limiting negative effects to your business reputation.

A PR program can help your business survive and come out on top in times of crisis. Here's a good example and something to keep in mind as you build your practice: several years ago, at the start of the Covid-19 pandemic, news reporters were on a "phishing" expedition trying to find natural healthcare providers who weren't following the law in our state. Reporters posing as a potential patient would email natural healthcare providers asking the provider if they had opposing views to the Covid-19 vaccination mandate and if they'd be willing to write a waiver. I remember receiving several emails to our naturopathic medical practice from reporters disguised as anti-Covid vaccination folks looking for a waiver. I remember telling my wife something was amiss and immediately trashing those emails. Something was up. Weeks later, a doctor in Washington was arrested and in the news for writing waivers and taking money for these "patients" and ended up paying a hefty civil and professional price.

Building and maintaining a positive reputation with your target audience and community will ultimately enhance relationships and ensure your brand integrity is intact. Next, I'll describe what goes into creating a public relations plan, then follow up with an example so you know what it might look like.

Building a Public Relations Plan

You can create your public relations plan as concisely or comprehensively as you desire. A public relations plan is a complete document outlining the strategies and tactics a business or practice will use to communicate with the public, promote its brand, and manage its reputation.

A typical PR plan frequently includes the following components:

1. <u>Situation Analysis</u> - This is a review of the current state of your business, including its market position, strengths, weaknesses, opportunities, and threats. Refer back to your marketing plan when you identified the SWOT for your business. By the way, how's that marketing plan coming along? Download your free Marketing Plan Guide at www.bradjohnsonmarketing.com and begin the process this week.

2. <u>Goals and Objectives</u> - You must create clear and measurable targets your business wants to achieve through PR, such as boosting brand awareness, improving reputation, or driving conversions and sales.

3. <u>Target Audience</u> - I can't overstate the importance of knowing whom you're directing your communications, identifying your targeted patients/clients/customer, along with understanding and identifying other key stakeholders that your business wants to reach with its messaging, such as customers, investors, employees, media, or policymakers.

4. <u>Key Messages</u> - It's essential to focus on your key messages and ensure they are clear, concise, and compelling.

5. <u>Tactics and Strategies</u> - Specific activities and approaches that the business will use to execute its PR plans, such as media relations, events, social media, content marketing, influencer outreach, or community engagement.

6. <u>Budget and Timeline</u> - A detailed plan for allocating resources and setting timelines for each tactic and strategy, including a budget, staffing, and metrics for measuring success.

7. <u>Evaluation and Measurement</u> - Establish a system for tracking and evaluating the outcome of your PR plan, including capturing metrics related to media coverage, social media engagement, website traffic, and customer feedback.

Now that we have a basic understanding of the elements of a PR plan, let's put this knowledge into action with a fictitious business. In this example, we envision a natural health supplement company that grows medicinal mushrooms called Myco-WellBeing, putting together its PR plan. Here's what that might look like:

<u>Situation Analysis</u> - Myco-WellBeing is a new startup business offering natural health supplements from medicinal mushrooms. It focuses on people with mild cognitive decline or wanting to enhance their mental functions. The company has a limited budget and staff. Still, it intends to establish itself as a leading provider of natural health supplements in the mycological sector in the local market.

<u>Goals and Objectives</u>:

- Increase brand awareness by 25% in the next six months.

- Drive traffic to the website by 30%.

- Generate at least five positive media mentions in local publications.

<u>Target Audience</u> - Men and Women aged 45-70 who are health-conscious, concerned about cognitive decline, and interested in natural remedies and treatments.

<u>Key Messages</u> - Myco-WellBeing is a trusted provider of natural health mycologic solutions that help people feel better, enhance cognition

and live healthier lives. We offer a wide range of medicinal mushroom products backed by science and supported by a team of experts.

Tactics and Strategies:

1. Media Relations - Pitch local journalists and bloggers on the health benefits of medicinal mushrooms to enhance cognitive function and offer bloggers or trusted influencers exclusive access to our products and services for reviews and features.
2. Social Media - Develop a social media campaign targeting our key audience, using influencers, engaging content, and promotions to build brand awareness and drive traffic to our website
3. Content Marketing - Produce high-quality blog posts, videos, and infographics that showcase our expertise and highlight the benefits of our products and services, and distribute them through our website, social media, and email newsletters.
4. Community Engagement - Host local events and workshops that offer free mycological consultations and natural health advice to practitioners and partner with local businesses and organizations to reach new audiences.

Budget and Timeline:

1. Media Relations: $5,000 over six months, starting in month 1.
2. Social Media: $1,500 over six months, starting in month 1.
3. Content Marketing: $1,000 over six months, starting in month 2.
4. Community Engagement: $1,000 over six months, starting in month 3.

Evaluation and Measurement:

1. <u>Media Coverage</u> - Track the number and quality of media mentions. Use media monitoring tools to measure the impact on brand awareness and website traffic. Important: the best way to track media mentions is to use Google Alerts. Google states, "Go to http://www.google.com/alerts. Type in the search query you want to monitor. Choose what type of results you want to follow (everything, news, blogs, video, discussions, or books). Choose how often you want to receive updates (as-it-happens, once a day, or once a week)" It's a great way to stay informed about who's talking about you or your business. Sign-up today!

2. <u>Website Traffic</u>- Use Google Analytics to track the number of visits, page views, and time spent on the site and measure the impact of each tactic on traffic and engagement. Many web hosting sites also offer analytics, allowing you to keep apprised of the same metrics.

3. <u>Social Media Engagement</u> - Monitor social media metrics such as likes, shares, and comments.

The truth is that nothing I've shared in this book is overly complicated and only requires a desire to build a profitable business/practice, tenacity to develop your planning documents, and the commitment to follow through with the execution of the plans. Setting a business up from scratch may seem like a significant challenge, but in reality, getting your first client - and getting them to return will be the most challenging issues you'll face; that's why it's so important (and why I keep harping on marketing plans) and for you to take a laser-focused approach and not get distracted by Doing Without Intention. Just think about the terrible content on social media, some of what you and I have both created and then consider what if we did a better job targeting our messages to our audience.

Getting the Word Out

Early in my career, I was the executive director of a nonprofit organization whose mission was to promote volunteerism, train volunteer coordinators, and help guide non-governmental organizations to best tap into the community to help recruit, retain, and recognize volunteers. It was satisfying work, but my academic training only briefly touched on how to direct a volunteer program and even less preparation for working with the media. Working with the media is a unique dance, as you're not paying them to help spread your message. That's advertising; instead, your goal as someone who likely hasn't been a public relations professional is to begin to build a relationship with the media (e.g., local reporters, editors, and news directors) and become a trusted source of information such that when they have questions about a topic where you're an expert - they call you!

Sure, it's easier to build a relationship with the media when representing a charitable organization. When getting the word out could mean the difference between life and death. In this role, I ran a volunteer center serving a large metropolitan area of three counties and more than 350 individual nonprofit agencies; some organizations were very tiny, with one staff member and others behemoths.

Without intending to sound too flippant, the news media members tend to be a cynical bunch. By the nature of their work, it makes sense that members of the news and entertainment media have a hardened shell. From experience, they are prone to quickly dismiss our outreach as a way to get something for free, so it's essential when you consider reaching out to the media with your news that it's newsworthy and timely and not seen as an appeal for free advertising. That's why it's salient to think like an assignment editor, news director, or writer when you plan to reach out.

It took some time to develop relationships with the writers, assignment, and news editors whose help I would need to send out a plea for volunteers or food for a local food bank; however, with persistence and a few phone calls or emails, I was able to build my list of contacts whom I could reach out to on a moment's notice for emergent calls to action. Remember earlier in the book, I discussed how persuasive messages tend to be more credible from a person who possesses "authority?" - become a trusted and authoritative spokesperson for your industry. It's important to remember building a trusting relationship is a slow process, and part of that means promptly responding to your media friends' calls or queries. It's typical when they reach out to you for help, they are on a tight deadline, and the writers don't have much time or patience to wait for you to get back to them tomorrow.

Media Tip 1 - Respond quickly to media requests and you'll soon become their go-to person

Not only do you need to be nimble in your ability to respond to their needs, but you may also find yourself having to be nimble. Take this example as an illustration. Living in Michigan, in my role at the volunteer center at the time, I was working with a local domestic abuse homeless shelter. I received a call from their volunteer coordinator during a frigid weather snap early one morning. She described an urgent need for cold weather supplies: blankets, coats and hats, and gloves for the moms and children in the shelter and was hoping I could help out.

The cold doesn't wait for anyone, so I immediately sprang into action and reached out to the news director at one of the local television stations with whom I'd developed a relationship to share and discuss the news I'd just learned. This was about 9 am on a Wednesday. The assignment editor asked if I could make it into the station for their noon news show, since someone booked had canceled, to talk about it on air. Absolutely! By the end of the day, blankets, cold-weather clothing, and cash donations were arriving at my office. In no time, we could distribute those items to the shelter. I can still recall the heartfelt note I received from one of the folks living in the shelter who'd written a letter of thanks saying, "I didn't want to ask for anything more than a safe place to stay, but me and my kids were cold, and now we sleep warm at night." Tears still well up in my eyes when I think of this moment.

Media Tip 2 - If invited to be interviewed or be live, on-air - go!

While it may seem daunting and a bit scary to field news reporter questions or be interviewed live on-air, it is also exhilarating and fun. Over the years, I have served as the on-air spokesperson for several nonprofits and businesses. As a result, I have learned essential tips and techniques to help make your debut smooth and enjoyable. While I enjoy the spontaneity and rush of a live news program and interview, I know it's not for everyone, so I'll share my secrets to a great news interview later in this chapter.

So how does a business get the media's attention without seeming like you want something for free?

The Fundamentals of Sharing News & Information

"A well-crafted press release can be a powerful tool in getting your message out to the world. It can help you generate media coverage, attract new customers, and build your brand." - Jeff Bullas

A business can use several different methods to communicate with the media when wanting to share the news. First, I'll touch on the four essential messaging approaches, beginning with the press release and finishing with a press pitch.

<u>Press Release</u> - I've frequently used press releases to gain the attention of my local media community and share timely information about upcoming events or other exciting announcements, such as a new hire

or the launch of a new product. A press release is a communication issued to the media to announce something newsworthy. For example, a press release can reveal a new product, service, or event or provide information about an organization or individual. Press releases are typically written in a standard format and follow a specific structure, including a headline, a lead paragraph, and additional information organized in bullet points or sections. I'll share a press release template below that you can use.

A press release is an efficient way to share news and information about your business with the media. For more than a decade, I worked in the wine industry as a marketing, communications, and public relations professional, and getting the attention of the media as a for-profit business may not seem like it'd be effective; however, I've had great success using the press release as a tool to capture their attention ultimately leading to print media coverage, news stories, and live on-air interviews.

<u>News Release</u> - A news release is similar to a press release but specifically focuses on providing newsworthy information to the media. We've used news releases to announce an event or philanthropic activity or to provide information about a business or individual. During the initial years of the Covid-19 pandemic, news organizations were focused on sharing "feel good" stories. The "hard news" took a slightly less prominent role; however, news departments are more interested in news content today. It's always good to keep current with local news trends by reading your local newspaper and noontime and evening news.

<u>Media Alert</u> - A media alert is a concise message sent to the media to alert them to an upcoming event or newsworthy occurrence. Media alerts are often used to inform the media of a press conference, product launch, or other important events. We'd send media alerts regularly

when I ran the marketing department for a premium winery. Because the business had a robust charitable component, we were often one of the first businesses to jump to action in the event of a community need. For example, when an international humanitarian crisis emerged, the winery launched into action by sending out a media alert, then reaching out directly to our wine club members, community members, and the general public. Within a week, our winery had collected more than four pallets full (4'x4'x4') of donated healthcare items, food, and clothing. It was a huge success!

<u>Press Pitch</u> - A press pitch is a communication, usually by email or in person, used to convince a journalist or media outlet to cover a story or event. A press pitch is typically more targeted and personalized than a press release or news release. It is focused on persuading the recipient to cover a specific story. Press pitches may include:

- Specific details about the story.

- Quotes from relevant sources.

- Other information intended to convince the recipient to cover the story.

As I've intimated, building trusting relationships with the media is crucial for any PR program. Pitching stories is an excellent way to stay front of mind to your media contacts, keeping in mind not to overdo it.

Now that we've outlined the fundamentals of news sharing let's jump right into how to create a press release that you can use as an exemplar moving forward. As you may recall, a press release is a written or recorded communication issued to the media to announce something newsworthy. First, let's jump into what goes into a press release, along with an example I created for my wife, Dr. Jill Johnson, ND of the Blue

Earth Medicines' naturopathic medical clinic giving you a visual model you can emulate.

How to Structure Releases

Each type of media communication will be slightly different due to the nature of the messages you are sending. Let's first dive into what's included in a Press Release:

Press Release - Here is a general outline of what you might include in a press release, along with a personalized example (figure 1):

<u>Headline</u> - A catchy and attention-grabbing headline that summarizes the main message of the press release.

Example: "XYZ Natural Medicine announces new product launch"

<u>Dateline</u> - The date and location where the press release was written.

Example: "Bothell, WA - January 16, 2023"

<u>Introduction</u> - A brief summary of the main points of the press release. This should be written in an engaging and informative way to draw readers in.

FOR IMMEDIATE RELEASE
JANUARY 16, 2023

CONTACT
Brad Johnson
Media Relations
10205 NE 185th St. #304
+318 329 1519
prosperpracticecoaching.com

BOTHELL NATUROPATHIC CLINIC ANNOUNCES NEW SERVICE
Blue Earth Medicine Clinic Breakthrough Treatment Arrives!

Bothell, WA - January 16, 2023 - Dr. Jill Johnson, ND of the Blue Earth Medicine clinic announced the launch of our newest service, herbal-infused hydrotherapy today. This innovative new natural medical approach is designed to revolutionize the way people heal from chronic stress disorders.

The Blue Earth Medicine herbal-infused hydrotherapy suite features a state of art hydrotherapy chamber, healing herbal-infusions, and a therapeutic session and is perfect for people suffering from chronic stress disorders. According to Dr. Jill Johnson, ND, "We are thrilled to bring this groundbreaking natural medical service to our community and can't wait to see how it helps our patients achieve healing relief from chronic stress." The Blue Earth Medicine herbal-infused hydrotherapy treatments will be available for patients on February 1, 2023 at our downtown Bothell and appointments are available online www.blueearthmedicine.com

Blue Earth Medicine is a leading naturopathic provider of nature-based treatments with a mission to heal the world one patient at a time. For more information, visit www.blueearthmedicine.com or contact Dr. Jill Johnson at info@blueearthmedicine.com

Stay tuned for more updates on the Blue Earth Medicine services and be sure to follow us on Facebook/Instagram for the latest news and service updates.

###

Yours Sincerely,
Brad Johnson
Media Relations
Prosper Practice Coaching, LLC

Example: "XYZ Natural Medicine Practice is excited to announce the launch of our newest service, herbal-infused hydrotherapy. This innovative new natural medical approach is designed to revolutionize the way people [insert relevant information here]."

<u>Body</u> - The main content of the press release, including all the details and supporting information. This should be written in a clear and concise manner, and should include quotes from relevant sources to add credibility to the information.

Example: "The XYZ Natural Medicine Practice herbal-infused hydrotherapy features [list features here] and is perfect for [target audience]. According to Dr. J. Love, 'We are thrilled to bring this groundbreaking natural medical service to our community and can't wait to see how it helps our patients/clients [achieve desired outcome].' The XYZ Natural Medicine Practice herbal-infused hydrotherapy treatments will be available for patients/clients [date] at [location] and appointments are available online [company website]."

<u>Boilerplate</u> - A brief company or organization description, including its mission and contact information.

Example: "XYZ Natural Medicine Practice is a leading provider of [products/services] with a mission to [company mission]. For more information, visit [practice website] or contact [name] at [email/phone]."

<u>Contact information</u> - The name, phone number, and email address of a person who can be contacted for more information about the press release.

Example: "For more information or to schedule an interview with Dr. J Love, please contact [name] at [email/phone]."

<u>Hyperlinks</u> - Links to any additional resources or information that readers might find helpful.

Example: "For more information about the XYZ Natural Medicine Practice, visit [link to product page]."

<u>Media assets</u> - Any images, videos, or other media that can be used to supplement the press release.

<u>End note</u> - A closing statement or call to action that wraps up the press release and encourages readers to learn more or take action.

Example: "Stay tuned for more updates on the XYZ Natural Medicine Practice services and be sure to follow us on [social media] for the latest news and service updates."

Remember, a press release aims to communicate important information to the media and the public clearly and concisely. You can create a compelling and professional press release by following this outline and including all the necessary information.

Now, let's shift our focus from a general press release to one focused on newsworthy items.

News Release

The template for News Releases is essentially identical to the press release. It differs primarily due to the type of content - newsworthy items. Below I have reiterated what goes into the release. You can use the example, in Figure 1, as a guide to putting your release together.

- [Name of organization] [Contact information, including Name, phone number, and email] [Date]

- FOR IMMEDIATE RELEASE

- [Headline]

- [City, State] - [Brief summary of the news, no more than a few sentences]

- [First paragraph: Expand on the summary and provide more detail about the news. Include any relevant background information and context.]

- [Second paragraph: Provide additional information and quotes from relevant sources, such as company executives or experts in the field.]

- [Third paragraph: Conclude the release with final thoughts or next steps. This could include information about plans or events related to the news.]

- [###]

- [Optional: Include a short bio or background information about the organization or individuals involved in the news.]

- [Optional: Include relevant images, videos, or other multimedia assets.]

Keep in mind that news releases should be concise, informative, and written clearly and straightforward. They should also be tailored to the audience and the media outlets receiving them.

News releases are a great way to communicate newsworthy messages to the media; however, sometimes your messaging doesn't need to be so "newsworthy" but still needs to be shared with news organizations.

Media Alert

A media alert is a brief, straightforward notification sent to media members to alert them about an upcoming event or news story. It is typically used to generate media coverage of the event or story, either through traditional outlets such as newspapers, television, and radio or through online platforms such as social media and blogs.

Here is a template for a media alert:

243

- Subject: [Brief, attention-grabbing description of the event or story]

- Date: [Date of the event or release of the news]

- Time: [Time of the event or availability of the news]

- Location: [Location of the event or availability of the news]

- Contact: [Name and contact information for a spokesperson or point of contact]

- Details: [Brief overview of the event or news story, including any relevant background information and any specific facts or highlights]

- Visuals: [Description of any visual elements that may be of interest to the media, such as photo opportunities, video footage, or graphics]

- Additional information: [Any additional details or instructions for the media, such as access instructions or embargo information]

It is essential to keep the media alert concise and to the point. It is intended to provide only the basic information needed to generate interest in the event or story. It is also paramount to include all necessary details, such as the date, time, location, and contact information, to make it easy for media members to follow up and get more information.

Press Pitch

Over the years, I've pitched many ideas to the media. As the name suggests, it's a pitch, like throwing a baseball over the plate - some are hits, and others miss. Of course, most pitches are misses, but regardless of whether a media outlet picks up your story idea or passes, your continued attempt shows persistence and demonstrates that you may be someone they can count on for another story yet to come.

A Press Pitch is characteristically an email message sent to journalists or media outlets to persuade them to cover a particular story or event. It is typically a brief, targeted message that aims to grab the recipient's attention and convince them to take action (such as writing an article or producing a segment about the story).

Here is a template that you can use as a starting point for creating your press pitch:

- <u>Subject Line</u> - Make the subject line of your email clear and compelling. It should give the recipient an idea of the email and why they should be interested.

- <u>Introduction</u> - In the first few sentences of your email, introduce yourself and your organization, and provide some context for the story you are pitching.

- <u>The Hook</u> - This is the most critical part of your pitch. It should be a short, attention-grabbing statement that explains why your story is worth covering. Be sure to highlight any newsworthiness or timeliness of the story.

- <u>The Story</u> - In a few paragraphs, provide more detail about the story you are pitching. Include relevant quotes, statistics, or other supporting information to help make your case.

- <u>The Angle</u> - Explain how your story differs from what has been covered in the past and why it is essential to the audience of the media outlet you are pitching.

- <u>The Offer</u> - Tell the recipient what you are offering, such as access to experts or sources, additional information, or images or video footage.

- <u>The Call to Action (CTA)</u> - End your pitch by clearly stating what you want the recipient to do (such as writing an article about your story or scheduling an interview with one of your experts).

Remember to keep your press pitch concise and to the point. Journalists and media outlets are often bombarded with pitches, so you want to ensure that yours stands out and is easily understood.

How to Build a Positive Working Relationship with Your Local Media

Building a solid working relationship with local media can help elevate you professionally and your practice by becoming a go-to source of expert knowledge about your field. There are several techniques that public relations professionals can use to build relationships with the media:

<u>Develop a Robust Media List</u> - Identify the media outlets and journalists relevant to your organization and the topics you want to cover. This can help you tailor your pitches and build relationships with the right people.

You can begin to build your list by reading your local newspapers, visiting news and information websites, and creating a file that contains the media outlet name, type of media (print, online, radio, television, etc.), website, contact name, email address, and phone number. After compiling a comprehensive list of media contacts, I'll build an email list for the media. Hence, it's simple when I want to send an email blast out. One thing that I've learned is that it's best not to blast the entire list out in a bulk email where all the other media members can see who's on your list; instead, it's important to send personalized emails to the news editor, assignment editor, reporter or writer of the media outlet you're sending.

<u>Be Responsive and Reliable</u> - It's worth reiterating that when journalists reach out to you for information or comment, make sure to respond promptly and provide the information they need. If you can't meet their deadlines, let them know immediately. Building a reputation for being responsive and reliable can go a long way in building relationships with the media.

<u>Build Personal Relationships</u> - Take the time to get to know the journalists you work with. This can involve meeting them in person, following them on social media, or having regular phone or email conversations. The more you understand their interests and needs, the better you can tailor your pitches and work with them.

Media Tip 3 - Keep the Relationship Professional yet Warm

As I've mentioned before, news media members take their roles seriously, and it's a fine line between being professional and being too cozy.

<u>Offer Value</u> - In addition to responding to media requests, try proactively offering value to journalists by providing them with relevant and timely information, such as press releases, blog posts, or expert quotes. This can help establish you as a valuable resource and build trust with the media.

Not so long ago, when I worked for a tourism-related organization, I attended a panel event in downtown Seattle where several travel writers discussed their process for story development and receiving cold pitches from folks and organizations. Of the several panelists, some were brusque, others snooty, and some just right. So afterward, I approached the "just right" ones and initiated a brief conversation, and we all shared business cards. The next day I sent an email thanking them for their contribution as part of the panel and letting them know more about the organization I represented. Not long afterward, one of the participants I'd met was working on a story for Red Tricycle, an online parenting magazine, and was looking for story leads. Unfortunately, for my client, I wasn't able to direct the writer to them; however, I did have an acquaintance - a local band/storyteller/artist that'd be a perfect fit, so I connected them both. The article was fantastic, and the writer and the unsuspecting recipient of my referral were delighted. The writer reconnected with me in a subsequent month and featured my client. Bam! That's a perfect synergy.

<u>Be Transparent and Genuine</u> - In your interactions with the media, it's essential to be transparent and honest. Don't try to spin a story or hide important information. This can damage your credibility and harm your relationships with the media.

<u>Say Thank-You</u> - I can't overstate this! Finally, be sure to show appreciation for your organization's media coverage. This can involve thanking journalists for their time and effort, sharing their articles on social media, or sending a quick note of appreciation. Thank you's can help build goodwill and strengthen your relationships with the media. This is super important: a thank you note is satisfactory but do not, under any circumstances, send anything of value (e.g., do not send cash, flowers, gift cards, a bottle of wine, etc.) - this will end your relationship. A brief thank-you note is sufficient.

Secrets to a Good Interview

One day, you'll be asked for an interview by a local newspaper, blogger, podcaster, or television station. Before my first interview, I was an avid *Letter to the Editor* writer, sending in opinion pieces monthly about volunteerism (you may remember, I ran a volunteer center a million years ago) in the hopes of getting my story printed and encouraging volunteerism. As expected, only some letters were published. Still, stories with a local focus and enough advance notice were often picked up. This simple letter-writing process opened the door for feature stories and built my credibility and authority as a subject matter expert. It was only a short time before I had reporters and news directors contacting me for interviews or requests to find other potential interviewees.

Over the years, I've had the opportunity to be an interview subject for many newspaper articles and stories, magazine articles, as well as local and national television broadcasts. Here is an example of when I was the interview subject. When I worked for a winery in the midwest several years ago, I sent a press pitch to our local television stations about some of our new award-winning wines. As a result, I was rewarded with two appearances during their morning news program. As the winery's external relations manager, I had the pleasure of waking up at 4:30 am getting to the television station by 5:30 am. Arriving before regular business hours, I was greeted with locked doors. After some time, they came to the door and welcomed me inside. The morning crew comprised two news anchors, a weather forecaster, a camera person, and a control room operator.

The news studio was crowded with three main areas, one large desk where the anchors read the news, a green screen area where the meteorologist stood, and another table where we gathered to discuss the wine. Inside the studio were three large television cameras on dollies, along with lots of lighting and cables.

The segments were brief, lasting at most about 3 minutes each. The caffeine-infused hosts were kind, full of energy, and launched into their teleprompter-fed script right on cue. It's interesting to get a behind-the-scenes look at the workings of a news studio and to be inside sharing our story, and a little surreal. Trust me, on a live broadcast; you cannot share everything you want, which is frustrating. But that's just how it is, so it's essential to be ready to go when they are, and it all happens quickly. Morning and noon news programs are filled with soft news stories and laughter. So, go with the flow, be articulate, and have fun.

Other times, I served as a coach to clients, owners, and winemakers, helping prepare them ahead of time, attending the shoot, and helping as I could. For example, I prepared a media pitch with our publicist a few years ago. I sent our local television stations a Thanksgiving wine and food pairing pitch. This project required our winery to connect with a local chef to prepare a made-for-TV Thanksgiving meal with our wines. We secured a chef willing to work for the cost of the meal and the media exposure. The barrel room was to be the location for the live broadcast because of the attractiveness of the backdrop. With a table full of gorgeous Thanksgiving food, the reporter and camera person arrived at 6:30 am, set up the connection with their live feed, and got ready to go live. Our on-camera people were the owners, winemaker, and chef. The publicist and I prepped our team with what to expect, and I cued them in on take-away messaging - the things I wanted the audience to hear - and off they went. Three live segments later, the show was done, and our winery received fantastic (and free) media coverage in a huge market. That's a win!

The previous section - *How to Build a Positive Working Relationship with Your Local Media* - should be kept in mind as you build a reputation.

Let's explore what it takes to be a Great interview!

<u>First, Relax</u> - Most of us will feel a sense of anxiety at the prospect of being interviewed, and that's, and it's perfectly normal. Remember that you are a subject matter expert and likely know much more about your area than the reporter, so take comfort in that.

<u>Be Prepared</u> - If you know the interview topic beforehand, familiarize yourself with the current knowledge around the subject. Sometimes the reporter or podcaster will send you a list of questions or topics ahead of time, and if that's the case, good for you. If so, look the questions over and practice answering - it's good if you have a friend or colleague you can use as a sounding board. If you only have a general idea about what you'll discuss, take stock of your knowledge in that area to prepare. Don't lose your mind over the interview, and it'll be brief. I understand that only some people love to be interviewed, photographed, or video recorded. Still, if you want to get the word out about your business or practice, then it's the price of admission. You've got this.

<u>Be Humble and Polite</u> - If you are lucky enough for someone to want to interview you, don't screw it up by being a jerk. Be gracious, grateful, and polite.

<u>Don't Over-Prepare</u> - it's good to know your stuff but don't get so rehearsed that it seems artificial. Be authentic - don't pretend to be someone you're not.

<u>Time Flies</u> - If you're being interviewed for a newspaper article, you can expect the interview to last only about 5-15 minutes. It goes very quickly. If you are being interviewed for a television story, expect the interview to last only 5 to 10 minutes. You'll spend more time watching

the reporter and camera person set up and take down than the interview itself.

<u>Have a Good Line</u> - News people love great sound bites! Not everyone can do this, but if you can, I'd recommend that you think like a news editor and plan to have a couple of good usable quotes in your answers. You may worry the reporter will want to "getcha" with trick questions or will use an awkward response from you. I've never had this experience; it's been the opposite. Most journalists want to write a good story with excellent sources. They are trying to impress their bosses, colleagues, and readers.

<u>Dress Nicely</u> - Many times, the interview will be via phone, so what you wear doesn't matter a whole lot; however, if your interview is live online, on video conference, or in person, it's a good idea to appear professional and put-together. There's no need to buy a new outfit unless you've been looking for a good excuse; then go for it!

<u>Have Fun</u> - It will appear in the article or interview if you love what you're doing. People pick up on that when you're grateful for the opportunity to share your knowledge. Enjoy the process, learn everything you can, and become their go-to person for the next interview opportunity.

<u>Be The Resource</u> - Whenever possible, I make it a practice to snag a business card from the interviewer to follow up with a "thank you note" and offer to be a resource moving forward. These business cards go into my media contact file, so I have a solid contact when I want to send a press pitch out.

REFERENCES

Ajzen, Icek & Fishbein, Martin. (1975). A Bayesian analysis of attribution processes. Psychological Bulletin. 82. 261-277.

Ajzen, I., & Fishbein, M. (1980). Understanding attitudes and predicting social behavior. Prentice-Hall, Inc.

Becker, M. H. (1974). "The Health Belief Model and Personal Health Behavior." Health Education Monographs, 1974, 2, 324-473.

Blount, A., Luszczynska, A., & Scholz, U. (2002). Locus of control and health behaviors: A meta-analysis. Journal of Behavioral Medicine, 25(3), 221-247.

Courneya, K. S., Karvinen, K. H., & Markland, D. (2002). Social cognitive theory and exercise behaviour change. Annals of Behavioral Medicine, 24(1), 90–98.https://doi.org/10.1207/S15324796ABM2401_11

DiClemente, R., Salazar, L.F., and Crosby, R.A. (2021). *Health behavior theory for public health: Principles, foundations, and applications*. Jones & Bartlett Learning.

DiClemente, C. C., & Prochaska, J. O. (1998). Toward a comprehensive, transtheoretical model of change: Stages of change and addictive behaviors. In W. R. Miller & N. Heather (Eds.), Treating Addictive Behaviors (2nd ed., pp. 3-24). Plenum Press.

Festinger, L. (1957). A theory of cognitive dissonance. Stanford University Press

Galloway RD. Health promotion: causes, beliefs and measurements. Clin Med Res. 2003 Jul;1(3):249-58. doi: 10.3121/cmr.1.3.249. PMID: 15931316; PMCID: PMC1069052.

Luszczynska, A., & Schwarzer, R. (2010). The role of self-efficacy and locus of control in health behaviors: a meta-analysis. Journal of health psychology, 15(6), 807-816.

Norcross, J. C., Krebs, P. M., & Prochaska, J. O. (2011). Stages of change. Journal of Clinical Psychology, 67(2), 143-154.

Pender, N. J. (1982). Health promotion in nursing practice. New York: Appleton-Century-Crofts. and updated in Pender, N. J. (1996). Health promotion in nursing practice. (4th ed.). Upper Saddle River, NJ: Prentice-Hall.

Prochaska, J. O., & DiClemente, C. C. (1983). Stages and processes of self-change of smoking: Toward an integrative model of change. Journal of Consulting and Clinical Psychology, 51(3), 390-395.

Prochaska, J. O., & Velicer, W. F. (1997). The transtheoretical model of health behavior change. American Journal of Health Promotion, 12(1), 38-48.

Prochaska, J. O., Norcross, J. C., & DiClemente, C. C. (2013). Applying the stages of change. Psychotherapy in Australia, 19(2), 10-15.

Rippe, J. M. (2015). Lifestyle medicine: a manual for clinical practice. Springer.

Strecher, V. J., Rosenstock, I. M., & Becker, M. H. (1986). The health belief model and personal health behavior. Health Education & Behavior, 14(1), 75-83.

About the Author

Brad's remarkable journey spans nearly three decades in the dynamic realm of marketing and communications. With unwavering dedication, he has honed his skills as a seasoned strategist and coach. His professional odyssey showcases diverse roles, including executive director positions for two nonprofits, board membership, and leadership in community-driven problem-solving initiatives.

As a college instructor, Brad empowered students to delve deep into the intricacies of human behavior through an array of psychology courses. Within the wine industry, his versatility shone through various roles, from cellar operations to winemaker assistant, where he deftly managed wholesale programs, supervised vineyard operations, and orchestrated unforgettable events, ultimately spearheading the growth of a robust wholesale program.

Brad's dynamic background encompasses pivotal marketing, community relations, public relations, and communications positions for wineries and nonprofit organizations. With nearly a decade dedicated to his marketing and communications strategist and coach role, Brad brings a treasure trove of knowledge and hands-on expertise to his clients.

His academic pursuits culminated in bachelor's and master's degrees from Central Michigan University. At the same time, his doctoral journey at the University of Idaho's College of Natural Resources has finely honed his mastery of communication theory and its practical applications.

Read more at https://www.bradjohnsonmarketing.com/.